In *Shepherding like Jesus*, ˍˍˍˍˍˍ ˍˍˍ ˍˍˍˍˍˍ a refreshingly countercultural book for pastors, pastors in training, and congregations who know something isn't quite right with leadership in the church today. With the Beatitudes as his guide, and with input from veteran pastors around the country, Hébert's work will do much to bring needed reform to pastoral ministry in America while encouraging pastors who have been wearied under the weight of far too many worldly expectations for their ministry.

Michael Pohlman, PhD, associate professor of Preaching and Pastoral Theology and chair, Department of Ministry and Proclamation, The Southern Baptist Theological Seminary, Louisville, Kentucky

Shepherding like Jesus is exactly the kind of book we need right now, and Andrew Hébert is the perfect person to write it. Bringing the Beatitudes to bear on our calling, Hébert reminds us of the character necessary for pastoral leadership and the spiritual power that comes with it. In a world that places emphasis on all the wrong things, books like this give me hope that we can be what God intends us to be. Read it well, brothers. It is food for your soul!

Jamie Dew, PhD, president, New Orleans Baptist Theological Seminary, New Orleans, Louisiana

I'm so grateful for this work that my friend, Andrew Hébert, has gifted the church. I believe *Shepherding like Jesus: Returning to the Wild Idea that Character Matters in Ministry* should serve as a new generation's "pastoral manual." Never have character and integrity in ministry been more important than they are today. In a culture that highlights giftedness and elevates celebrity, Andrew calls us back to the center and speaks to what really matters and what is ultimately most effective—ministering from the overflow of a heart that loves Jesus and is committed to humbly following him. It's filled with inspiration and practical application, and also includes personal reflections by some of the most respected and seasoned pastors from across the country. I wish this had been available for me to read when I was first called to ministry at age seventeen. I'm grateful it's available to all of us in ministry now.

Jarrett Stephens, senior pastor at
Champion Forest Baptist Church, Houston, Texas,
and author of *The Always God: He Hasn't
Changed and You're Not Forgotten*

Indeed, character does matter in pastoral ministry. Without returning to the primacy of reflecting Christ in everyday living and leading, the desired impact of pastoral ministry will be greatly diminished. This is exactly what Andrew Hébert addresses in *Shepherding like Jesus* as he challenges followers of Christ to reflect the attitudes contained in the Beatitudes. This book will force reflection and bring conviction in the leader's life.

Michael S. Wilder, PhD, dean of the
Terry School of Educational Ministries
and professor of Educational Ministries, Southwestern
Baptist Theological Seminary, Fort Worth, Texas

Andrew Hébert is 100-percent correct in observing that our church cultures often undervalue the role of character in pastoral ministry. No one would deny its importance, of course. But if we value Christlikeness in our pastors as much as we ought, we will often be swimming against the current! This helpful and edifying book, rooted in both the Beatitudes and real-life pastoral reflections, will help us recover and pursue this desperately needed focus. I highly recommend it for all—especially pastors, elders, and all who serve the local church in some capacity.

Gavin Ortlund, PhD, senior pastor,
First Baptist Church of Ojai, California, and author of
*Finding the Right Hills to Die On: The Case for
Theological Triage* and *Theological Retrieval for
Evangelicals: Why We Need Our Past to Have a Future*

Everything mentioned in the Bible about pastoral qualifications is about the character of the pastor. That is why I am excited about Pastor Andrew Hébert's new book, *Shepherding like Jesus*! This book should be required reading for every pastor and preacher who desires to shepherd like Jesus. Each chapter of the book challenges pastors to be men of character. As a bonus, at the end of each chapter there are "Pastoral Reflections" to further equip pastors in the ministry. Thanks, Andrew, for helping us shepherd like Jesus.

Fred Luter, senior pastor, Franklin Avenue
Baptist Church, New Orleans, Louisiana, and former
president, Southern Baptist Convention

Character is key to leadership. No one can lead effectively without integrity, and this is especially true for pastors. This book identifies and addresses key areas of your ministry and personal qualities that will pay big dividends if you carefully tend to them and bring huge consequences if you don't. Looking at the attributes and ministry of Jesus as the ultimate example, Andrew Hébert has written a book every pastor needs to read and keep in his library.

Kevin Ezell, president, North American Mission Board (SBC), Alpharetta, Georgia

This book gets at the guts of pastoral ministry. In ministry, it does not matter how competent you are, how much capacity you have, or even if you feel called to the pastorate, if you lack the character of a pastor. Andrew Hébert, in this timely book, reminds us of the essential truth in Christian ministry: character still matters. He admits that this is not a novel idea but rather a retrieval of something old that is often forgotten—a retrieval that I believe is necessary.

J. T. English, PhD, lead pastor, Storyline Fellowship, Denver, Colorado, and author of *Deep Discipleship*

True pastoring is more than just preaching—it is a multifaceted ministry that calls for multidimensional pastors. Andrew Hébert helps us see that Jesus calls for pastors to live the multitude of Beatitudes from the Sermon on the Mount. *Shepherding like Jesus* is the kind of book that can renew a pastor's ministry and, more importantly, their own discipleship with the risen Christ.

J. A. Medders, director of assessment, Acts 29 Network, host of The Acts 29 Podcast, and author of *Humble Calvinism*

In an age where charisma, eloquence, and talent draw crowds and prompt many to "aspire" to pastoral ministry, Andrew Hébert challenges us to return to the most important aspect of the pastor's life: his character and holiness. I pray this book stirs your affections and compels you to check your heart and motivations as you seek to shepherd the flock like Jesus.

Félix Cabrera, executive director, Baptist Convention of Puerto Rico, director, SEND Puerto Rico, and pastor, Iglesia Bautista Ciudad de Dios, San Juan, Puerto Rico

SHEPHERDING
LIKE JESUS

The author's proceeds from the sale of this book will be donated to the Lottie Moon Christmas Offering for International Missions and the Annie Armstrong Easter Offering for North American Missions.

ANDREW HÉBERT

SHEPHERDING
LIKE JESUS

Returning to the Wild Idea that
Character Matters in Ministry

B&H
PUBLISHING
NASHVILLE, TENNESSEE

Dedicated to my wife, Amy, "a lily among the thorns," without whom I would not be who I am, where I am, or what I am.

And to my children: Jenna, Austin, Mackenzie, and Brooklyn. I love you each so much. May you come to know and love Christ for who he is, the One who is full of grace and truth.

Contents

Contributors

Russ Barksdale is the retired senior pastor of The Church on Rush Creek in Arlington, Texas.

Mac Brunson is the senior pastor of Valleydale Church in Birmingham, Alabama.

Michael Catt is the retired senior pastor of Sherwood Church in Albany, Georgia, and executive producer of *Facing the Giants* and *Fireproof.*

Steve Dighton is the retired senior pastor of Lenexa Baptist Church in Lenexa, Kansas.

Hance Dilbeck is the president and CEO of GuideStone Financial Resources in Dallas, Texas.

Jimmy Draper is the president emeritus of Lifeway Christian Resources.

Nathan Lorick is the executive director of the Southern Baptists of Texas Convention in Grapevine, Texas.

Doug Munton is the senior pastor of First Baptist Church, O'Fallon, Illinois.

Clint Pressley is the senior pastor of Hickory Grove Baptist Church in Charlotte, North Carolina.

Juan Sanchez is the senior pastor of High Pointe Baptist Church in Austin, Texas.

Robert Smith Jr. is the Charles T. Carter Baptist Chair of Divinity at Beeson Divinity School in Birmingham, Alabama.

Bobby Worthington is the pastor of Lake June Baptist Church in Dallas, Texas, and the associate professor of missions and evangelism and director of applied ministry at Criswell College.

Preface

In March 2020, a global pandemic emerged that brought our country to a standstill. The economy came to a screeching halt, local businesses shut down, and churches across the nation closed their doors for three months in light of public health concerns. Amid the shutdown, God laid it on my heart to redeem the time by writing a book for pastors. The words flowed quickly as I put onto paper the things that have been in my heart and mind for some time now.

My prayer for this book is that it will refresh and encourage the hearts of pastors and other church leaders. I fear that sometimes the model of pastoral ministry that gets the most press in the American evangelical scene is a model with which most pastors do not resonate and cannot replicate. "Celebrity pastor" culture is harmful to our vocation as pastors. It is also exhausting. For a generation of pastors who feel like the expectations for their ministry do not reflect biblical norms, my hope is that this book will be a healing balm. A biblically faithful pastor does not have to look like the megachurch pastor down the street. His church does not have to triple in size for him to be counted among God's faithful shepherds. He does not have to get ahead or compete with other churches or be a "visioneer," whatever that means. But he *must* be a man shaped and formed by Christ. I hope this book extends both a high calling for every pastor to reflect the character of Christ in the pastoral task and great encouragement that our righteousness and character are produced by Christ alone.

I want to give a few special acknowledgments. First, special thanks are in order for the pastors who contributed pastoral reflections at the end of each chapter. These are men who reflect pastoral character in their ministries and have been a great example to me. I want to thank my father, Allen, for reading drafts of early chapters and providing helpful editorial feedback. He and my mother, Becky, consistently encouraged me during this project. I cannot thank my wife, Amy, enough. She read and edited the entire book. She has been a constant cheerleader and faithful friend for as long as I have known her. I am so thankful for her friendship. I'm thankful for each of my children: Jenna, Austin, Mackenzie, and Brooklyn. They provided needed fun and distraction when I had writer's block. I strive for my public ministry and private life to be consistent so that they will come to love Christ because they see his life in mine. They are one of the great gifts and joys of my life.

Special thanks go also to the man who first stirred up within me a love for the Sermon on the Mount. Dr. Roy

Metts is the best teacher I have ever had. As the long-time professor of Greek and New Testament at Criswell College, he taught me to love the Scriptures. What's more, he shared his life with me (1 Thess. 2:8). I deeply appreciate his mentorship and friendship over the years.

I want to thank several people at Lifeway and B&H Publishing Group. I am so grateful for Ben Mandrell and his encouragement in this work. Without him, you would not be seeing this book in print as it is. The B&H team is one of the best in the business. Devin Maddox, Taylor Combs, and my editor, Logan Pyron, are men whose input and collaboration made this book possible. Thank you all.

Finally, I want to thank the church members who have called me "pastor" through the years. Being a shepherd of a local church is a great calling and privilege. For the congregations I have had the blessing of pastoring through the years and which have, in turn, blessed me and my family, I am thankful. Fairhaven Baptist Church, Direct Baptist Church, Taylor Memorial Baptist Church, and Paramount Baptist Church have taught me so many valuable lessons about faith and ministry. Because of their love and support of our family through the years, my wife and kids have been blessed and not held bitter thoughts about the local church. Thank you.

Andrew C. Hébert
Amarillo, Texas

FOREWORD

What Is "Success" in Pastoral Ministry?

Much has been made of the importance of God's call on a man's life to preach the gospel and to shepherd the church of the living God. That call is an indispensable requirement for one who occupies the role of pastor. However, we may have misunderstood that call! Our call from God is to come into a relationship with him. The pastor serves out of that relationship with God. No man should attempt to become a pastor who does not live in a personal and vital relationship with God. God is more concerned about who we are *with* him than in what we do *for* him.

The absolute necessity of a man's deeply personal relationship with God is a nonnegotiable requirement of the pastor. The principles revealed in these pages apply to you and will enable you to be God's voice to those who hear you as you draw upon your personal relationship with God himself.

In 1879, in his remarkable book *The Pastor: His Qualifications and Duties*, Hezekiah Harvey wrote an amazing paragraph:

> The men who deal with spiritual things must themselves be spiritual. . . . Spiritual force comes from within, from the hidden life of God in the soul. It depends not on mere outward activities, but on the divine energies acting through the human faculties, God working through the man, the Holy Ghost permeating, quickening all the powers of the preacher, and speaking His voice to the souls of the people. The soul's secret power with God thus gives public power with men, and the mightiest influences of the pulpit often flow from a mere utterance of man: there is in it a power more than human.[1]

In other words, *character really matters.* The pastor cannot make it *for* God until he is real *with* God! The world of Hezekiah Harvey was much different from our world today. Life was simple in the midst of two industrial revolutions. Modern travel and technology were nonexistent. Knowledge was expanding rapidly with few of the conditions we live in today. Harvey's words certainly applied to the world of 1879, but think about how much more they apply in the midst of the many distractions, turmoil, and advancements of the world today.

Today's pastor faces insurmountable challenges far beyond the abilities of human wisdom and energy. The pastor cannot lead people to God in his own gifts. Dependence upon and intimacy with God must be the experience and practice of the pastor. The call to preach is a sacred trust from our sovereign God to those he knows he can trust.

What kind of man can God trust? *The secret lies in one's character.* He must be a man of integrity, purity, and honesty, with compassionate love for others and a passion for the truth of God. In short, it requires a man who lives and preaches according to God's standards alone!

Andrew Hébert has taken the most remarkable sermon ever delivered and brought it down into the pastor's heart and life. It was delivered by our Lord to more than five thousand individuals on a Galilean hillside. It begins: "After he sat down, his disciples came to him. Then he began to teach them, saying . . ." (Matt. 5:1b–2). Thousands heard that sermon, but it was directed to those disciples who would be used by God to change the world as they delivered his message.

That is what this book is all about: God-called men taking his message of hope to a desperate world. These words we call "the Beatitudes" are placed before those uniquely called of God to go from his presence to deliver his message. That includes you and me!

Be blessed as you read. Be transformed as you apply this message from our Lord Jesus Christ. Your assignment is unique. Your strength is inadequate. Your abilities are limited. But out of your relationship with God, empowered by his Holy Spirit within you, you will become all he called you to be through the wisdom and power he channels through you!

Dr. Jimmy Draper
President Emeritus, Lifeway Christian Resources

Introduction

Poor in spirit. *Broken. Humble. Hungry. Sympathetic. Pure. Reconciling. Enduring.* These are not the words that describe the typical picture of the modern-day "successful" American pastor, but these are the words Jesus said should characterize the lives of his twelve disciples, the men who would lead the church after he ascended into heaven. In the Beatitudes of the Sermon on the Mount, Jesus paints a clear picture of eight attitudes his disciples should embrace if they expect blessing. They are backwards, upside down, surprising, and not at all what typical American congregations expect of their leader.

No, if we were to write the Beatitudes today, they would look something like this:

> Blessed are the rich, for their needs will
> be met.
> Blessed are the bold and the beautiful, for
> they will be well liked.
> Blessed are the self-promoters, for they will
> be noticed.

> Blessed are the spiritually self-satisfied,
> for they already have everything they
> need.
>
> Blessed are the ruthless, for they will get
> ahead in life.
>
> Blessed are the shrewd, for they will have
> the upper hand.
>
> Blessed are the conquerors, for no one will
> get in their way.
>
> Blessed are the comfortable, for they will
> never experience trouble.

Many modern-day pastors cut a different image from the biblical picture of a local church shepherd. We are dreamers, visionaries, catalysts, ambitious, thought-leaders, influencers, motivators, and change-agents. Much time is spent crafting and sustaining our image, broadening our reach, and extending our platform. Poor in spirit? Mourning? Humble? Not so much. In many circles, the image of what a pastor is or does looks nothing like the picture Jesus paints for his disciples of the character that marks citizens of his kingdom.

This book is a call to rebel against much of what our culture understands pastoral leadership to be and return to being the Christ-shaped shepherd God has called us to be. It's a challenge to swim against the current of much of what passes for pastoral life these days. It's an invitation to recover the most essential element of pastoral ministry: the character of Christ.

I have good news for you. You do not have to be a "catalytic leader" or a "bold visionary" to be a good pastor. You do not have to be a dynamic communicator or a church growth guru. The most essential component for successful pastoral ministry is not ministerial competence or leadership capacity, but character. Representing Christ well as a pastor means reflecting his character in and among his flock. If you succeed in the area of character, then you can be a successful pastor even in the absence of other gifts or abilities. But if you succeed in church growth, preaching, and leadership but fail in character, you have failed in what matters most.

On February 10, 2019, the *Houston Chronicle* published the first part of a six-part series entitled "Abuse of Faith," a heart-wrenching exposé of sexual abuse in Southern Baptist churches. The investigation traced the stories of more than seven hundred victims, reaching back twenty years, and unveiled an unsettling pattern of sex abuse that, until now, had largely been kept quiet by some churches and church leaders within the forty-six thousand churches of the Southern Baptist Convention (SBC).

Widespread sexual abuse within the Roman Catholic Church had been exposed a number of years before, but for many evangelicals, the *Houston Chronicle* exposé hit much closer to home. It revealed the fact that several hundred pastors had used their positions of spiritual authority to manipulate and abuse those under their pastoral care. Though many of these pastors were appropriately convicted for their egregious crimes, some of their abuse remained unknown to the churches they served. And in the worst cases, some of the abuse was known but kept quiet. This allowed these pastors to accept pastoral positions in other churches, going from church to church over the years and perpetuating their abuse with other victims.

This scandal rocked the Southern Baptist Convention, causing the SBC president, J. D. Greear, to publicly announce new policies for the denomination to keep this from happening again. Churches, seminaries, and the denomination's Ethics & Religious Liberty Commission immediately began thinking about how to educate pastors and church members to think more carefully and intentionally about the safety of every person within the reach of their ministries.

Across the denomination, the revelation of this scandal was a wake-up call. It didn't primarily reveal a public relations challenge for the world's largest Protestant denomination. It revealed a *character* problem. How could men who claimed to represent God perpetuate these horrifying acts of abuse upon members of God's family?

On the heels of this ecclesiastically earthshaking story, several national headlines broke describing pastors and other Christian leaders across the country who were resigning their positions of leadership due to accusations of extramarital affairs and other inappropriate behavior. There is a *character* problem in the American church today. Many pastors' gifting has taken them where their character cannot keep them. The character of Christ in the life of the pastor is the most needed aspect of pastoral ministry, but in many cases it is also the most neglected.

There has never been a time in church history when so many resources have been available to pastors on church leadership, church growth, preaching, and many other practical topics. If you are experiencing a challenge or a question about how to do something, there is a book, an expert, a consultant, a seminary professor, a "thought leader," or some other guru just around the corner who can give you a quick how-to on whatever problem you face. As someone with a doctorate in leadership, I am definitely *for* these resources and find them necessary and helpful. But I find that many pastors are discouraged when they attend conferences or pick up yet another book telling them how to do ministry in ways most pastors cannot identify with and can never replicate. What if what the church needs most is not another book on the "mechanics" of leadership and church growth? What if what the church *really* needs today is a return to something more basic; namely, a recovery of the character required of spiritual leaders?

The greatest pastoral imperative I have is to adopt the attitude of Christ in my life. It is the most necessary and foundational aspect of pastoral ministry, much more important than making hospital visits, preparing church budgets, or even preaching great sermons. It is the one thing without which ministry cannot succeed.

That is what this book is about. I've written about what modern-day pastoral leadership books do not write about enough. It's the missing ingredient in many pastorates and the reason so many pastors crash and burn before crossing the finish line. Sadly, embracing the character of Christ means going against the grain of much of what pastoral leadership has become in twenty-first-century churchdom.

But how do we know what the character of Christ should look like in the life of a pastor? I believe that Jesus' Sermon on the Mount, and the Beatitudes in particular, contain a portrait of the character of Jesus, the very character he wants to shape into our lives as Christians and as Christian pastors. This book is not an attempt to provide new insight about how to get your church to double in size or how to become a preacher people can't refuse to hear. Instead, this book is a return to something very old. This is not a book about the competency of a pastor or his capacity, but his character. It is a fresh application of the greatest sermon ever preached to the lives of today's pastors and church leaders. It is a primer on the character of Christ in the life of the pastor.

As we consider these matters together over the pages to come, I have invited a few other pastoral voices into the conversation. After each chapter in this book, I've included a "pastoral reflection" contributed by a number of experienced pastors I deeply respect. I am so thankful for these wise and godly pastors whose ministries have influenced and benefited my own. I want to give special thanks to Jimmy Draper, Russ Barksdale, Steve Dighton, Nathan Lorick, Robert Smith Jr., Doug Munton, Michael Catt, Bobby Worthington, Juan Sanchez, Clint Pressley, Mac

Brunson, and Hance Dilbeck. The insights they share on each chapter's theme are invaluable.

I do not write as a perfect man or a perfect pastor. What I write about here is as much aspirational for me as anything else. The Beatitudes are life-changing, and they are verses I seek to live out in my daily life. But I am still very much "in process." What I share in these pages, I hope will be an encouragement to you as it has been to me. I want to be a faithful pastor who crosses the finish line of faith and ministry and hears, "Well done, good and faithful servant!" (Matt. 25:23). I hope that is your desire as well. If it is, my prayer is that what you read in this book will encourage you to keep running the race with endurance, laying aside the sin that so easily besets us, and "[keep your] eyes on Jesus, the pioneer and perfecter of our faith" (Heb. 12:1–2). As a fellow pilgrim in the pastoral path, I urge you to look to Jesus' example and his exhortations in the Sermon on the Mount as the starting place for understanding our pastoral task and calling.

CHAPTER 1

Pastoral (Bad) Attitudes

*For the shepherds are stupid: They don't seek the
LORD. Therefore they have not prospered, and
their whole flock is scattered.*

—Jeremiah 10:21

Pastors are normal people. The shepherd of God's
flock is still a sheep himself. As a pastor, I am not a
"father" but a "brother," a real brother who is part of the
same dysfunctional family as the rest of God's children. I
struggle with the same things everyone else does. Pastors
wrestle with sin, doubt, failure, discouragement, temptation, heartache, depression, anger, bitterness, pride, greed,
jealousy, ambition, hurt, loneliness, and burnout. I have
often told people in counseling situations that there is little
they can tell me that will surprise me—not only have I
heard it before, but in many cases I have been there myself!

The truth is that we have all been there—wanting to throw in the towel, to let a church member know what we really think, and to take the "mask of ministry" off for a minute. We are tired of always having to be "on" when we are in public. I will admit that I have been frustrated at times when I am at the grocery store or eating at a restaurant with my family on my day off, and a church member comes up and sits down at the table to share some "concerns" he has about something happening at the church. I do not always have the most sanctified thoughts. We all have bad attitudes at times.

Sometimes, though, these bad attitudes extend far beyond small frustrations to sinful thoughts, actions, or desires. And sin in the life of a pastor, like sin in the life of any believer, is deadly.

The "Black Ice" of Ministry

As an undergraduate student at Criswell College, I served as a bi-vocational pastor of a church about an hour and a half north of the Dallas-Fort Worth Metroplex. I lived in Dallas and commuted back and forth on the weekends to pastor this small-town church. One weekend we experienced a snowstorm that left the roads icy. Since my hometown is Houston, I had about as much experience driving in ice as I did milking a cow—which is to say, none. As I was making the trip up for the weekend, I hit a patch of black ice that I couldn't see but was most definitely there. Before I knew it, my truck began to spin out of control, doing a series of 360-degree turns on the interstate. God protected me that day. Many don't survive that kind of unforeseen danger.

The challenges of pastoral ministry are often unforeseen but always deadly. Only one out of ten pastors who start out as a pastor will finish that way.[1] Whether through moral failure or spiritual burnout, many pastors do not survive the "black ice" of ministry.

While an extensive list of pastoral dangers would be impossible to summarize here, there do seem to be some temptations "common to man" (1 Cor. 10:13 NKJV) that especially endanger pastors.

Fame

The Irish poet Dallán Forgaill once wrote: "Riches I heed not, nor man's empty praise." I have found, however, that in ministry it is easy to heed man's empty praise. The temptation of fame can be fatal in ministry. It is a subtle seduction because it can take different forms and is often masked with righteous aims. We want more "likes and shares" of our online sermons so that "we can reach more for Christ," but how many times is there a small dose of prideful arsenic mixed in with our righteous intentions? We all have a desire to be recognized and to be significant. God created us to have God-directed ambition. But sin always twists God's good gifts. The desire for fame often looks like ambition or recognition wrongly directed.

Fame can take the form of ambition. Too many pastors are constantly looking over the ministry fence to see if the grass is greener at another church. Some pastors are obsessed with "climbing the ministry ladder" and, sadly, use their church as a stepping-stone to get to a ministry assignment that is more appealing. Rarely do pastors leave their current churches for smaller or less influential churches. God always seems to call us to larger, more prominent places. Could it be that ambition is creeping into our interpretation of God's will for our next ministry step? Ambitious pastors are blind to the goodness, grace, and gifts of God. They find discontentment with where God has called them and what he has called them to do. I wonder at times if our obsession with "bigness" does not cloud our view of God's kingdom work all around us that is happening in smaller ways and places.

Fame can look like a desire for recognition. We all want to be recognized as talented and gifted. We enjoy hearing a compliment and get hurt when we hear a criticism. Both responses can reveal just how much pride and the desire to be recognized have seeped into our souls. Do you feel as joyful when others are recognized as you are when you receive recognition? Do you feel slighted when you do not receive public or private praise? These may be indicators that you desire fame more than you realize. We sometimes believe our own hype and listen too much to our own internal PR spokesperson.

Pastors sometimes want to be recognized as the "man in charge." As we were loading into the car after church one day a few years back, one of my kids asked me: "Daddy, are you the boss of the church?" I remember laughing as I thought about how far from the boss of anything any pastor really is. Yet if we are not careful, the "boss of the church" mentality can creep into our mindset as pastors. There is a big difference between "shepherd" and "chief shepherd," and it is best not to confuse the two. When things do not go our way or when someone pushes back against our leadership, we realize just how much the idol of recognition has crept into our lives.

The "boastful pride of life" (1 John 2:16 NASB) is one of the three original sins of the garden of Eden. Paul warns that a pastor should "not be a new convert or he might become conceited and incur the same condemnation as the devil" (1 Tim. 3:6). Fame is a hunger that will never be fully satisfied. If you are not content with what God has given you at this present moment, you will likely never have enough to be fulfilled. Paul said that he "didn't seek glory from people" (1 Thess. 2:6). The desire for fame, recognition, and the pursuit of prideful ambition—these are ministry killers.

Infidelity

Sexual temptation is real. Giving in to this temptation will render a pastor's ministry dead on arrival. One of the danger zones for pastors is treating women we are not married to as anything other than "sisters, with absolute purity" (1 Tim. 5:2 NIV).

Billy Graham famously determined never to be alone with a woman who was not his wife. He would not eat a meal or ride in a car alone with another woman. He would not even walk into a hotel room without first having a staff member check it to make sure there was not a woman hiding in a closet, waiting to catch him in a compromising situation. This protected Dr. Graham's ministry from public reproach and left him uncompromised in his ministry.

We must be so careful in how we relate to the opposite sex. In our friendships, in our pastoral counseling, in our visitation, in our social media interactions, appropriate relationships can quickly become inappropriate if we do not embrace the response Joseph took in temptation: run!

Sexual temptation is a problem in the church. We have all heard of too many pastors who have dropped out of ministry because of moral failure. George Barna discovered a few years ago that 57 percent of pastors and 64 percent of youth pastors admitted to struggling with pornography either currently or in the past.[2] And that's just the number of pastors who were willing to admit it. Studies show that 37 percent of pastors admit to having an inappropriate sexual relationship with a church member.[3] The articles in the *Houston Chronicle* about sex abuse in the church demonstrate that the admonition to be sexually pure cannot be taken seriously enough. The ripple effects of sexual sin extend far beyond any one of us to include our wives, our children, our children's friends, the church, and the community, and can even create regional or national headlines. Lust, flirtation, pornography, adultery, sexual abuse, and sexual immorality of any and all kinds are deadly dangers for pastors.

Fighting

Perhaps no other ministry danger is more personally draining than church conflict. Several thousand churches close every year, and many of them close because of division and fighting within the church.

Satan loves nothing more than dividing, distracting, and discouraging Jesus' church. Nothing will zap a church of its spiritual vitality or steal a pastor's joy faster than a church fight. Some church members love drama. In fact, they are bored if there isn't something to gossip or fight about. It is sad but all too true.

I clearly remember the first conflict I experienced as a pastor. A member was upset at how long my sermons were. (He had a point.) He called a secret committee meeting to which I was not invited and sought to rally support against me. A few months later he tried to stir the pot again because he disagreed with my interpretation of a biblical text about the end times. I remember being so discouraged that he would try to turn church members against me that I seriously contemplated quitting and going into some other field. Little did I know that it would just go downhill from there. I have experienced conflict in every church I have served. Some are harder than others, but none are more difficult to witness than watching staff members gather people together to leave the church and start something new down the road.

Unfortunately, in a fallen world, conflict is inevitable where two or more are gathered together. But fighting becomes deadly, and the hurt within churches becomes more intense when the pastor gets involved. Pastors should always take the high road—there is less traffic there. But from time to time, pastors give in and join the fight. At times they will even throw around their weight to try to win. Sadly, if a pastor has to remind the church that he is the pastor, it usually means he has lost his leadership in that congregation. In our digital age, this fighting spirit may even show up outside the walls of the church and end up on the walls of the pastor's social media pages. I am sad to say that I have participated in a number of these unhelpful social media feuds from time to time myself.

This is not to say that the pastor should *never* participate in a fight. A pastor friend once encouraged me during a difficult time of church conflict in this way: he said that a pastor should rarely draw his sword, but if he does, he ought to make sure he is the last one standing and then be willing to stay long-term to put the broken pieces back together. There are times when a pastor is called to "contend for the faith" (Jude 3). There are times when a pastor should drive out wolves from the flock (Titus 1:9–14). There are hills worth dying on. The problem is when we make mountains out of every molehill and are eager to fight. There is a difference between standing for what is right and going around picking fights or engaging in church disputes with the wrong spirit and the wrong aims.

Paul says that a pastor must not be "a bully but gentle, not quarrelsome" (1 Tim. 3:3).

When a pastor has a combative spirit and is eager to put on the boxing gloves every time there is a differing point of view, not only does he fail to exemplify the character of Christ, but it almost always spells the end of his ministry within that church or, at a minimum, ends the effectiveness of his ministry. When we fail to be agents of unity, we do not represent Christ well.

Finances

Finances can present a world of problems in ministry. As those who lead ministries that operate entirely upon the generosity of God's people, pastors have to walk carefully through the minefield of personal and church finances. Financial missteps affect not only the church's life but also the reputation of Christ in the community.

Finances present multiple challenges and dangers for pastors. Perhaps the most obvious and egregious is the embezzlement or misappropriation of church funds. We have all heard of churches who have suffered because of this. Sometimes it happens through an elaborate scheme where the pastor steals the church's money a little at a time or a lot all at once. Sometimes the crime is less blatant. Perhaps the pastor uses a church credit card for nonapproved personal expenditures, getaways, or personal golf games. Whatever the case, this is stealing.

Another financial danger is when a pastor mismanages the church's finances. This is not always intentional, but it does happen. Perhaps it is due to ignorance, negligence, or risky stewardship practices. Financial mismanagement is a land mine. Few pastors are prepared to steward the budget of the church by themselves. Committees provide great protection in this regard. Committees can keep us from making unintentional, but still unwise, mistakes. I heard of one pastor whose church was in hard financial straits, so he took church money to Las Vegas and gambled it away in an attempt to multiply it and save the church with this one last-ditch effort. Truth is sometimes stranger than fiction. A practice one pastor suggested to me many years ago and that I have embraced ever since is never to touch the money. Even if a church member comes up to hand me their tithe check, I won't take it. I will simply direct them to put it in the offering box or in the mail. I want to remain above reproach. A reputation takes a lifetime to build but only a moment to lose.

Financial misappropriation and mismanagement are more common than any of us want to admit. Yet most pastors will not experience either of these land mines. Much more common is the land mine of financial greed. Brothers, we must be so careful about our motivations in ministry. Paul says that he did not have "greedy motives" (1 Thess. 2:5). Peter exhorts the pastors of the Diaspora to "shepherd God's flock . . . not out of greed for money but eagerly" (1 Pet. 5:2).

We all have the responsibility to provide for our families (1 Tim. 5:8). I want to make enough money to provide for my wife and kids, to be generous to the Lord and to others, to save for the future, and to enjoy the good gifts God allows us to enjoy. But if that is *why* I'm doing what I'm doing, then money is my master, not Jesus. If I am in the ministry for the money, my motives are mistaken. The truth is, there is no amount of money the church could pay me to make up for the stress, headaches and heartaches, lost sleep, interrupted vacations, and conflict that go with the territory of being a pastor. If my motivation is to be compensated adequately for the work I do as a pastor, I am going to be disappointed. My motivation must be more than money.

Our motive in ministry should be to love the Lord, the Word, the church, and the lost. A pastor friend once humorously told me why the church does and does not pay him. He said the church does not pay him to preach or to make hospital visits. He loves preaching and loves people and would do those things for free. He said the church pays him to manage the darn staff. I'll leave that one right there. We do it all for the Lord.

We must be aboveboard in all things related to finances. Few things hurt the witness of the pastor or the church in the community more than the pastor's misappropriation, mismanagement, or misplaced motivation in regard to money. The love of money truly is the "root of all kinds of evil" (1 Tim. 6:10). A lack of integrity in the area of finances is a clear and present danger in ministry.

Fatigue

Leadership is a high-stress calling. There are no two ways about it. Pastors have all the stresses of any leader with the added weight of spiritual burdens. The hazards of the job include physical, mental, emotional, relational, and spiritual fatigue. Many pastors walk around burned-out without even realizing it, having become so accustomed to perpetual exhaustion that they do not even notice it anymore. It often takes a physical or mental breakdown before pastors realize how tired they are. Sometimes pastors do not realize how susceptible to sin they are in this fatigued state until they make a life-altering decision to give in to one temptation or another in a moment of exhausted vulnerability. We often do not realize what the weight of ministry has done to our souls until it's too late.

Few pastors take care of their own souls in the midst of taking care of the flock. Many lack disciplined rhythms of spiritual, relational, and physical health. The busyness of doing the Lord's work can sometimes crowd out the intentionality of being in the Lord's presence. Most pastors identify with Martha much more than they do Mary.

Some of the fatigue comes from the inescapable responsibilities of pastoral ministry. Sermon preparation, for instance, is a round-the-clock responsibility. I have jokingly said that preaching is in some ways like pregnancy—you give birth to the sermon on Sunday morning and then find out you are pregnant again on Monday morning! There is no real way to leave this work at the office. I carry the sermon around in my mind and heart all week long, at all times of the day and night. And that's just sermon prep! The constant needs of the people for counseling, weddings, funerals, hospital visits, the need to lead the church staff well, coordinate with church committees, work with church deacons, fulfill responsibilities to the community and the denomination can all be overwhelming and never-ending. There has never been a time in my ministry when I have laid my head down on the pillow at the end of the day and thought, *I finished everything I needed to do today.* There is always more to do. It is exhausting, and there is no way of getting around it.

Some of the fatigue associated with ministry is what ministry does to us, but some of it we do to ourselves through sinful action or perhaps sinful inaction. An unwillingness to be disciplined physically or spiritually often leads to spiritual burnout that is no one's fault but the pastor's. Some pastors have a "hero complex" where they will not take the time off that the church offers for them to replenish their own souls and invest much needed away time with their families. Failing to observe Sabbath rest is as much a sin as failing to observe the Commandments not to commit adultery or murder. A failure to rest is its own type of unfaithfulness, but the mistress is work. It is its own type of murder, where the pastor is killing himself to work. He is also killing his own joy and the joy of his family. John McCallum describes this experience well:

I never had a complete breakdown . . . but I often carried around a low-level depression. I often did my work without enjoying either the work, the people, or God in the process. I do not think the people I have served picked up on that very much. I wore the mask pretty well. In retrospect, however, I realize that in my weariest seasons I deprived the church, my family, myself, and the Lord of my best ministry and my deepest joy. I was serving Jesus as if he was a slave-master rather than a shepherd, as if he was more Pharaoh than friend.[4]

Friends, this is more common than most church members will ever know. Fatigue is often a gateway drug that weakens the pastor's defenses against other sin. Fatigue may reflect sinful habits that don't reflect the character of Christ who "often withdrew to deserted places and prayed" (Luke 5:16). Jesus modeled a rhythm of work and rest that pastors should, but often do not, imitate.

A Call to the Character of Christ

In light of these temptations, what we need most is not another book on the how-tos of ministry. We need nothing less than a return to the character of Christ. Fame, females, fighting, finances, fatigue—these are just a few tools Satan uses to derail pastors from their God-given ministries. These temptations, like all others, do not create character problems but simply reveal the character problems that were already there. As pastors, and as believers, we are called to more than this. We are called to the character of Christ. Embracing Christ's character is the essence of what it means to be a pastor.

There are many ways of thinking about pastoral ministry. One common way to think about the pastorate is through the lens of *logos*, *ethos*, and *pathos*. *Logos* in ministry has to do with the content of the message we preach, the "good deposit" (2 Tim. 1:14) that has been entrusted to us and which we are to entrust with others. *Pathos* in ministry is about whether the preacher believes the message he preaches. *Ethos* focuses on the believability of the preacher. Is his life consistent with what he preaches? Does he walk the walk or just talk the talk?

Much has been written about the *logos* and even the *pathos* of ministry, but not enough has been written about the *ethos* of ministry. The ethics of pastoral ministry relates primarily to the pastor's character. Does the life of the pastor reflect the character of Christ?

There is no better place to go than Scripture to understand what the character of Christ in pastoral ministry should look like. And there is no better place in Scripture to look than the Sermon on the Mount, the greatest continuous section of Jesus' teaching recorded in Scripture. In the Sermon on the Mount, we have a clear picture of the character Christ wants to form in the life of every believer, but especially in the shepherds of Christ's flock. We are going to journey into what I believe is the most foundational paragraph of the most famous sermon ever preached to see how the character of Christ can take shape in the life of the pastor.

Ministry Mistakes and How to Survive Them

– Russ Barksdale –

One of my favorite movies is Remember the Titans, *based on a true story about when the school board in Alexandria, Virginia, integrated the high school and its football team in 1971. Predictably, there was a lot of tension between the black and white players. It all came to a head when the white captain, Gerry, was complaining to the black cocaptain, Julius, about the attitude of the black players. Julius responded: "Attitude reflects leadership." He said a mouthful when he uttered those words. The statement stunned Gerry, who stopped blaming others and began taking on the responsibility to raise the levels of his leadership and attitude.*

I cannot overemphasize the absolutely critical component of attitude in life and ministry. In fact, building on Julius's response to Gerry, I would say, "Attitude is EVERYTHING!"

In my personal experience, nothing gets me into more trouble quicker than having a bad or unhealthy attitude about something or someone. I could write a one-hundred-volume work on the times a wrong attitude has hindered my life and ministry! All because I didn't have the depth of relationship with Jesus and the full understanding of his perspective.

There was something else I didn't have: humility. I remember reading a book on humility by Andrew Murray when I was in my mid-twenties. His premise was that if pride is the root of all sin, then humility must be the root of and the highest of all virtues. I certainly saw the merit in his argument and agreed with him. What a difference it would have made in my life if only my mental understanding of that great truth had sunk deep into my soul.

We make ministry mistakes because of our prideful attitude. I have a strong leadership gift, and I've been proud of it! It led me to burnouts, struggling seasons in my marriage, autocratic decision-making, unnecessary church squabbles, unhealthy personal financial decisions, and a whole slew of other problems. I know that Jesus was "tempted in all things—yet without sin" (Heb. 4:15 NASB). Well brothers, I confess to you I have been tempted in most things and sinned just about every time.

Here's how to survive ministry mistakes: "Have this attitude in yourselves which was also in Christ Jesus, who, although He existed in the form of God, did not regard equality with God a thing to be grasped, but emptied Himself, taking the form of a bond-servant, and being made in the likeness of men. Being found in appearance as a man, He humbled Himself by becoming obedient to the point of death, even death on a cross" (Phil. 2:5–8 NASB).

The application for us is to not "think more highly" of ourselves (Rom. 12:3 NASB): listening to others' opinions, knowing that good decisions require full vetting, taking time to build consensus rather than push our plan through, preparing sermons like it was our last one rather than coasting on our merits, valuing every interaction with people on Sunday morning whether they're our biggest giver or we don't even know their name, guarding ourselves and avoiding situations that could lead to adulterous behavior, handling our money and the church's money as if Jesus was watching every penny (he is!), and accepting the fact that we are not bulletproof.

We. Will. Break. And our brokenness will hurt the people we love the most, the worst. Intimacy with Christ is key. Keep going to that well. Get that living Water and Bread of life every morning. He'll get you through!

CHAPTER 2

Pastoral Beatitudes

When he saw the crowds, he went up on the mountain, and after he sat down, his disciples came to him. Then he began to teach them, saying . . .

—Matthew 5:1–2

I am not a handy man. I respect those who seem to know intuitively how things work and have the ability to fix pretty much anything. Growing up, I don't ever remember seeing a repairman come to our house to fix something because my dad is one of those do-it-yourself heroes who could have his own TV program. Not me. I usually spend more money trying to fix the mistakes I made while trying to fix something in my house than I would have if I had just called a repairman in the first place.

However, in the last few years this has begun to change. I have discovered that for some basic home repair work, I can look up instructional videos on YouTube. I can search for whatever home project there is and usually find more videos than I have time to watch. I like that. Even though I am not very good at it, I feel like I can watch someone show me how to do it and imitate what they do.

As a pastor, I have felt the same way about ministry, especially when I was first starting out. I do not feel particularly good about the many aspects of what I do, but if I can watch someone else do something well, then I can slowly pick it up and figure out how to do it myself.

Many books have been written to help pastors understand how to do ministry. Most of these how-to ministry books focus on practical aspects of the pastorate, such as preaching or leadership. They help us with the logos and pathos of ministry. There are more books of this sort than a pastor can read in a lifetime.[1]

But long before a pastor is ready to preach a sermon or lead a church, he needs to be taught something more foundational. What pastors really need, what they need more than step-by-step instructions on how to preach great sermons or lead great churches, are how-to instructions on the character of Christ. There is no such thing as effective ministry without the fundamental presence of personal character in the life of the pastor. All the natural and developed gifts in the world cannot make up for a deficit of Christlike character.

Brilliant in the Basics

In his memoir entitled *Call Sign Chaos*, General Jim Mattis recounted that he used to drill into the Marines under his command that they must be "brilliant in the basics."[2] He discovered over time that the greatest mistakes on the battlefield were usually attributed to a soldier's inability to perform the basics well. I want to be brilliant in the basics of ministry. I am less concerned with the bells and whistles of modern church life than I am the nuts and bolts of biblical church life. I want to do the basics and do them well.

"The basics" for a pastor begin with a pastor's character. Some fundamental character traits or attitudes must be pursued diligently in order to succeed as a pastor in the things that matter most. These do not relate primarily to how to accomplish the basic functions of ministry (such as how to conduct a wedding or a funeral or how to make a hospital visit) but relate to the character necessary to minister well, how to minister for the long run, and minister in such a way as to bring Christ glory.

We need to be taken to the seminary of the chief Shepherd to learn the ethos of ministry, the personal character required of a pastor in order to represent Christ well among his people and the world. What pastors need more than anything—more than preaching ability, leadership gifting, or pastoral skill—is Christlike character. When Paul lists the qualifications necessary for pastors, he does not primarily describe the competencies pastors should have but the character they *must* have. In fact, of the pastoral qualifications mentioned in 1 Timothy 3:1–7, only two relate to competency (the ability to teach in verse 2 and the ability to manage the church in verse 5) while more than ten have to do with the pastor's personal character. Christlike character is the starting place for pastoral ministry.

But where can we go to see a how-to on developing the character of Christ? I'd like to suggest that there is no better place and no more practical instruction in all of Scripture to discover the requisite character needed in ministry than the greatest sermon ever preached, Jesus' Sermon on the Mount (listed in its fullest expression in Matthew 5–7), and particularly the first section of that sermon, the Beatitudes. The purpose of this book is to explain how the Beatitudes can be applied to the life of the pastor so that he can develop Christlike character. Before we dive in to our study, I want to briefly introduce you to the sermon.

The Greatest Sermon Ever Preached

The Sermon on the Mount is the fullest and most extensive section of Jesus' teaching recorded in Scripture. It is the crown jewel sermon of Scripture. In both its substance and its structure, it is a masterpiece. By way of giving some background to the sermon, let me draw your attention to several of its unique features.

The general flow of the sermon in its macro structure is as follows. The *first movement* of the sermon is Matthew 5:1–48, where Jesus explains how to move from a state of unrighteousness ("poor in spirit," v. 3) to true righteousness (the righteousness that exceeds that of the scribes and Pharisees, v. 20). The *second movement* of the sermon is 6:1–18, where Jesus explains how to exercise the righteousness of the kingdom, specifically by warning against a kind of "show righteousness" that exercises spirituality in order "to be seen." The *third movement* of the sermon is 6:19–34, which is a parenthetical amplification of his teaching about giving and fasting, anticipating the audience's objections to what he has said in 6:1–18. The *fourth movement* of the sermon is 7:1–12, where Jesus picks up where he left off in 6:1–18 to continue his explanation of how to exercise the righteousness of the kingdom, this time warning against self-righteousness. The *conclusion and invitation* of the sermon is 7:13–27, where Jesus leaves the audience with two ways or two choices. He contrasts two gates and two ways in 7:13–14, two trees and two fruits in 7:15–23, and two builders and two fates in 7:24–27.

Some of the major themes in the sermon include a description of our sin nature as well as our need for dependence on the Lord to fill us with righteousness (5:1–6); an explanation of what the righteous life looks like (5:7–7:29), touching on the themes of murder (5:21–26), adultery (5:27–30), divorce (5:31–32), truth telling (5:33–37), going the second mile (5:38–42), loving our enemies (5:43–48); the importance of the spiritual practices of prayer, fasting, and giving, all done without the desire to be recognized (6:1–18); an exhortation about wealth and worry (6:19–34); a warning against judgmentalism (7:1–6); an invitation to come to the Lord with brazen boldness to meet our spiritual needs (7:7–12); and a description of what happens when someone follows or rejects the Lord (7:13–29).

New Testament scholar Charles Talbert divides the structure of the sermon into ten sections and summarizes its content in a series of sentences that beautifully capture the major themes and overall message of Jesus' teaching:

1. Matthew 5:3–12

    Congratulations to those whose vertical and horizontal relations are right for they will receive eschatological blessings.

2. Matthew 5:13–16

    Be who you are for the glory of God.

3. Matthew 5:17–20

    Since Jesus came to realize the intent of the Law, following him yields true righteousness.

4. Matthew 5:21–48
    a. vv. 21–26
        Be a person who neither breaks relationships nor fails to restore broken ones.
    b. vv. 27–30
        Be a person who does not violate another's marriage partner, either by act or by thought.

    c. vv. 31–32

        Be a person who does not violate the indissoluble marriage bond.

    d. vv. 33–37

        Be a person who is not deceitful but is truthful in all relations.

    e. vv. 38–42

        Be a person who does not retaliate but who returns good for evil.

    f. vv. 43–48

        Be a person who does not exclude your enemies from the love shown to your friends.

5. Matthew 6:1–18

    a. vv. 1–6, 16–18

        Be a person who avoids ostentatious displays of piety, because they are directed to the wrong audience.

    b. vv. 7–15

        Be a person who avoids babbling in prayer, because it assumes an incorrect view of God.

6. Matthew 6:19–24

    Be a person for whom wealth is not a functional deity but who lets God be God.

7. Matthew 6:25–34

    Be a person who does not suffer from debilitating anxiety but who trusts in God's providential care.

8. Matthew 7:1–5

> Be a person who does not condemn others for their
> flaws until having first corrected one's own.

9. Matthew 7:6–12

> Be a person who does not fail to discern the differ-
> ence between good and bad, using the wisdom given
> by God, and does not fail to act appropriately.

10. Matthew 7:13–27

> Be a person whose life is in line with God's will and
> Jesus' words, who will not be led astray by spiritual
> leaders who fail to do God's will, even if they have a
> proper Christological confession and mighty works in
> Jesus' name.[3]

As you can see, these features show that the com-
prehensive content of the sermon as well as its beautiful
structure make it a masterful message. It is the greatest
sermon ever preached.

But the sermon's most outstanding feature is that this
is the character of Christ on display. He fully embodies the
ethic of the kingdom to which he calls his disciples. The
sermon reveals the norms and expectations for kingdom
citizens. We are called to embrace the posture Jesus himself took: meekness, mercy, purity, peacemaking, etc. The
Sermon on the Mount is "a portrait of Jesus."[4]

For Christians to experience a life of God's full blessing, we must embrace the Sermon on the Mount as the

normative expectation for our life, our attitudes, and our behavior. Helpfully, the message of the Sermon on the Mount can be grasped just by understanding its introduction in Matthew 5:1–12.

Introducing the Introduction: The Beatitudes

The introductory section of the Sermon (vv. 1–12), commonly known as "the Beatitudes," is actually a summary of the entire sermon. In the Beatitudes, we see in embryonic form every one of the characteristics of Christ that the sermon will bear out. The introduction is the sermon in shorthand; the Beatitudes are the Cliffs Notes to the Sermon on the Mount.

In fact, every part of the Sermon on the Mount is connected to one of the eight Beatitudes. There is a chiastic structure in the sermon that flows from the Beatitudes.[5] The chiasm looks like this:

A 5:3 Blessed are the poor in spirit
  B 5:4 Blessed are those who mourn
    C 5:5 Blessed are the humble
      D 5:6 Blessed are those who hunger and thirst for righteousness
        E 5:7 Blessed are the merciful
          F 5:8 Blessed are the pure in heart
            G 5:9 Blessed are the peacemakers
              H 5:10–12 Blessed are the persecuted

H' 5:13–16 Salt and light

G' 5:21–26 Anger and reconciliation

F' 5:27–37 Lust, divorce, and remarriage; keeping your word

E' 5:38–6:4 No revenge, no hate, and no "paraded" acts of mercy

D' 6:5–18 How to seek in prayer, no parade in prayer or fasting

C' 6:19–34 Treasure in heaven, the single eye, no anxiety

B' 7:1–6 No judgment, recognize our faults, avoid the unrepentant

A' 7:7–11 Ask, seek, knock

Conclusion 7:13–29 The either/or

Another way of thinking about this chiastic arrangement is that the Sermon on the Mount is essentially an elaboration of the eight Beatitudes, in reverse order. The beatitudes are related to the other sections of the sermon as follows:

8. Persecuted (5:10–12)   Salt of the earth (5:13)
Light of the world (5:14–16)

7. Peacemakers (5:9)   No anger or insult (5:21–22)
Be reconciled (5:23–24)
Settle with enemy (5:25–26)

6. Pure in Heart (5:8)   No lust (5:27–30)
No remarriage (5:31–32)
No broken oaths (5:33–37)

5. Merciful (5:7)	No revenge (5:38–42)
	No hate (5:43–48)
	No "paraded" mercy (6:1–4)
4. Hunger/thirst for righteousness (5:6)	No parade in prayer (6:5–8)
	How to seek in prayer (6:9–15)
	No parade in fasting (6:16–18)
3. Humble to inherit earth (5:5)	Treasure in heaven (6:19–21)
	The single eye (6:22–24)
	No anxiety (6:25–34)
2. Mourners (5:4)	No judgment (7:1–2)
	Recognizing our faults (7:3–5)
	Avoid the unrepentant (7:6)
1. Poor in spirit (5:3)	Ask, seek, knock (7:7–11)
Conclusions: The "either/or"	Two gates and ways (7:13–14)
	Two trees and fruits (7:15–23)
	Two builders and fates (7:24–29)

In other words, if you understand the Beatitudes, you understand the whole message of the sermon. There may be no more important set of verses in Scripture for understanding what the ethos of a believer, or that of a pastor, should look like than Matthew 5:1–12.

There is an important logic to the order in which the Beatitudes are given. At a macro level, Matthew 5:1–6 describes a process, while Matthew 5:7–12 describes the result of that process. You could say that the first six verses describe kingdom attitudes while the last six verses describe kingdom actions that flow from those attitudes.

At a micro level, the Beatitudes describe what a life of "hunger[ing] and thirst[ing] for righteousness" (v. 6) looks like. The first beatitude says that those who are "poor in spirit" are blessed (v. 3). This means that you must recognize your own spiritual poverty. When you do that, it leads you naturally to the second beatitude which describes mourning or brokenness over sin. As you are broken over your sin, you come to the realization of the third beatitude, the importance of becoming humble, realizing that you do not have what it takes and you are now ready for God to do for you what you cannot do for yourself. Once you take the posture of humility, you are ready for the fourth beatitude, to hunger and thirst for the righteousness only Jesus can produce in your life. What does that righteousness look like? Jesus gives four further beatitudes describing the actions of the righteous: you become a person of mercy toward others, a pure person, a peacemaker, and someone who endures trials for the sake of the kingdom. Each of these eight beatitudes are then expanded in the rest of the Sermon on the Mount. This is the character Christ intends to form in all who follow him. This is the blessed life.

The word *beatitude* finds its origin in the Latin word *beatitudo*, which means "blessed." It comes from the repetition of the Greek word *makarioi*, which is usually translated as "blessed" or "happy." Thus, "the Beatitudes" refers to the "blessed are" section of the Sermon on the Mount. These *makarisms* find their parallel in the Old Testament in passages such as Psalm 1:1–3:

> How happy is the one who does not walk in the advice of the wicked or stand in the pathway with sinners or sit in the company of mockers! Instead, his delight is in the LORD's instruction, and he meditates on it day and night. He is like a tree planted beside flowing streams that bears its fruit in its season, and its leaf does not wither. Whatever he does prospers.

Living a life "blessed" by God means having God's approval on your life. Max Lucado says it is having "the applause of heaven."[6] The Beatitudes describe the posture a believer should take to live a life approved by God. We can also say that this is a description of what it takes to be a pastor who is approved by God.

A. M. Hunter says, "The Beatitudes of Jesus describe the character of the men who, living under God's Fatherly Rule made manifest in Jesus, enjoy . . . happiness even here and now, though its perfection belongs to the heavenly world."[7] When you embrace the ethics of the Beatitudes, you experience a taste of the future in the now, a taste of heaven on earth. A beatitudinal life is the life of the age to come lived in the midst of this present, evil age. In short, the Sermon on the Mount and the Beatitudes in particular describe the blessing of the true righteousness associated with life in God's kingdom, the righteousness without which it is impossible to enter the kingdom (Matt. 5:20), and the righteousness that only Jesus can produce in us (v. 6).

Pastoral Beatitudes

The Beatitudes should interest every follower of Christ. But they should interest pastors in particular for this reason: Jesus preached the Sermon on the Mount not primarily to the crowd but to the small, committed group of men who would lead the Christian movement into the future. The sermon was given primarily to the twelve disciples and only secondarily to the crowd. In Matthew 5:1–2, Jesus, seeing the crowds, withdraws with his disciples who gather around him as he goes up the mountain. The text specifically says, "he began to teach *them*," referring to the disciples who came to him (v. 2, emphasis added). This teaching was primarily directed to *leaders*. If Jesus ever had a leadership manual, this is it. These are not merely Christian beatitudes; they are *pastoral* beatitudes.

Jesus is teaching the norms of the kingdom to the men who will lead the church and ignite the explosive growth of Christianity. That means that the sermon, while applicable to every believer, has particular importance and application to pastors and other Christian leaders. There may be no more direct and relevant instruction regarding the character Christ wants to form in the Christian leader than in Matthew 5:1–12. Truly, the beatitudes describe the spiritual attitudes pastors must embrace if they want to represent the chief Shepherd well among the flock of God.

"Have This Attitude among Yourselves"

I have always wanted to be a pilot. It's still on my bucket list. On my birthday a number of years ago, my wife purchased one flight lesson as a gift. It was incredible. I learned about flaps and ailerons, yoke and rudder, and lift, thrust, drag, and weight. I also learned about an airplane's *attitude*. The attitude of an airplane refers to its position relative to the horizon.

As pastors, we ought to consider our position relative to the person of Christ. Paul said, "Adopt the same attitude as that of Christ Jesus" (Phil. 2:5). Do we look like Christ? Do our lives exemplify Christlikeness? Do people smell "the fragrance of Christ" when they are around us (2 Cor. 2:15)? The eight beatitudes give us a way to measure our attitudes and our character relative to the character of Christ. A pastor is called to be poor in spirit, broken over sin, humble, hungry and thirsty for righteousness, merciful, pure in heart, a peacemaker, and one who is willing to persevere through persecution. This is the character of Christ in the life of the pastor.

The "Well Done" in Ministry: Why Character Is Necessary to Pastor Well for the Long Haul

– Steve Dighton –

I have observed in the Christian life the emphasis has been more on how a person begins rather than how he finishes. This truth is seen not only in the pew but in the pulpit as well. Unfortunately, the goal of "finishing well" has greatly diminished throughout the evangelical world. According to Pastoral Care, Inc., only one pastor out of ten finishes in the ministry.[1] So the attrition rate is truly alarming. Still the Bible is replete with continual calls to persevere, to endure, to be steadfast, and to discipline ourselves for godliness. There are multiple reasons for this disconcerting drop-out rate, but the reason for the overwhelming majority is that the leader compromised his character and fell prey to "the sin that so easily entangle[d] him" (Heb. 12:1).

Many have believed that to be a high-capacity leader one has to be charismatic, insightful, or have the ability to communicate vision or some "wow" factor. While these traits are desirable, they become wood, hay, and stubble when personal integrity is compromised. Character is the quintessential trait for everyone called of God.

*I retired as the founding pastor of Lenexa Baptist Church
in 2016 after serving twenty-six years in the suburbs of Kansas
City. When I packed my office and handed the keys to the new
pastor, the greatest satisfaction was not that I had labored to
relocate the church, had built four buildings, begun five new
campuses, or left the church debt free. No, it was that I had
finished well. There was great satisfaction that I had completed
what God had called me to do and now I was leaving a legacy
of faithfulness.*

*Was it easier for me than for the overwhelming majority of
those who didn't finish well? Maybe it was; I can't say. What
I can say is this: I cherished God's call on my life, and I labored
under his sovereignty and his sufficiency. I kept my integrity
intact, and I finished the work God had for me.*

*As I reflect on some needful helps to finish well, three safe-
guards come to mind.*

*First, keep your wife close and understand the dynamic
nature of the need to serve together. If your wife does not see
this as essential, it will be difficult for you to finish well. I
have been married forty-nine years to Dr. Mary Dighton, a
retired dentist. Mary always worked outside the home and still
gave priority to supporting me, standing with me, and serving
alongside me. It made my ministry successful and sustainable.
The last fifteen years at Lenexa Baptist Church, I preached
multiple services, and she sat beside me in every service. When
there is a genuine devotion to each other by the pastor and his
wife, it builds security and trust with the people at church. The
Scripture is true: "Two are better than one, because they have a
good reward for their labor" (Eccles. 4:9 NKJV).*

Second, find contentment in the simple and glorious fact that God has called you to shepherd his people. So feed them, lead them, and plead for them. Do not let people, problems, or predicaments rob you of the promised joy in serving (John 13:17). So my counsel is to stay, pray, and labor tirelessly where God has uniquely placed you. Every destination has its challenges. Contentment will never be found merely in a relocation.

Third, there is no substitute for integrity, so be truthful, be honest, be faithful to your wife and to your family, live above reproach, flee sexual immorality, and lead by example. Do not become weary in well-doing that you might finish this monumental race (Heb. 12:1–3).

CHAPTER 3

The Spiritually Impoverished Pastor

"Blessed are the poor in spirit, for the kingdom of heaven is theirs."

—Matthew 5:3

When my wife and I got married, we were very young and very poor. We were so poor, in fact, that just a couple of weeks before we said, "I do," I actually overdrafted my bank account. A bank overdraft is when you try to draw more money out of your bank account than it actually holds. I received an alarming overdraft notice from the bank, letting me know that I did not have enough resources to pay for what I owed on a particular purchase. It was not a great way to start a life of wedded bliss!

"Blessed are the poor in spirit," Jesus says (Matt. 5:3). The first beatitude in the Sermon on the Mount confronts us with an unsettling truth: we are spiritually bankrupt. We do not have what it takes.

Being "poor in spirit" does not mean embracing financial poverty. It does not mean going around with a sort of downcast spirit in order to be pitied by others. D. A. Carson defines it accurately:

> Poverty of spirit is the personal acknowledgment of spiritual bankruptcy. It is the conscious confession of unworth before God. As such, it is the deepest form of repentance. It is exemplified by the guilty publican in the corner of the Temple: "God, be merciful to me, a sinner!" It is not a man's confession that he is ontologically insignificant, or personally without value, for such would be untrue; it is, rather, a confession that he is sinful and rebellious and utterly without moral virtues adequate to commend him to God. From within such a framework, poverty of spirit becomes a general confession of a man's need for God, a humble admission of impotence without him.[1]

We observe spiritual poverty in several ways. First, we do not have what it takes for our salvation. We cannot save ourselves. Our account of righteousness is empty. "All have sinned and fall short of the glory of God" (Rom. 3:23). "There is no one righteous, not even one" (Rom. 3:10). We teach our children the ABCs of becoming a Christian; the first step is to "acknowledge I'm a sinner." We are spiritually impoverished because we are sinners. We do not have enough in the spiritual bank to pay for our sin.

Members of Alcoholics Anonymous begin their twelve-step program by acknowledging that on their own they have no power over alcohol. Acknowledgment is the starting point for the journey of discipleship. *I can't. He can. So I'm going to let him.* Later in the Sermon on the Mount, Jesus tells his disciples unless their righteousness "surpasses that of the scribes and Pharisees, you will never get into the kingdom of heaven" (Matt. 5:20). But if you start with verse 3, you realize that the true righteousness of the kingdom is something you do not and cannot manufacture on your own. We need God to give it to us. We need God's *saving* grace. Grace is God giving us what we do not deserve by doing for us what we cannot do for ourselves. Some have said that grace is *God's Riches at Christ's Expense.* Christ is the one who purchases our redemption because our spiritual bank account is bone-dry. Recognizing our need for God's saving work in Christ is what it means to be poor in spirit.

Second, not only do we not have what it takes for our salvation, we do not have what it takes for our sanctification. Not only do we need God's saving grace, but we also need his *sustaining* grace. We need God to do what we cannot do for ourselves both in justification *and* in sanctification. You aren't justified by grace and then sanctified by works. No, it is all God's grace. You aren't expected to pick

yourself up by your own spiritual bootstraps each morning
and try to be the best Christian you can be. Instead, God's
Spirit is active in our lives to *empower* our obedience, to
do for us what we cannot do for ourselves because of our
spiritual poverty. Through the "sanctifying work of the
Spirit," we grow in our maturity in Christ (1 Pet. 1:2). It's
the difference between trying to swim across the ocean
and taking a cruise ship. In one way, you are trying to do
an impossible task on your own. But in the other way, God
does all the work and carries you along for the ride. God's
Spirit animates our lives and enables us to be and do what
God desires.

Third, not only do we not have what it takes for our
salvation or for our sanctification, we do not have what it
takes for ministry. William Willimon reflects on the complex challenges that face every pastor:

> The pastoral ministry requires a wide
> range of sophisticated skills—public speak-
> ing, intellectual ability, relational gifts,
> self-knowledge, theological understand-
> ing, verbal dexterity, management acu-
> men, sweeping floors, moving folded metal
> chairs, serving as a moral exemplar, and
> all the rest. No wonder failure is always
> crouching at the door.[2]

Pastoral ministry is overwhelming. If we are going to
be pastors who are shaped into the likeness of Christ, we
must begin by acknowledging our spiritual bankruptcy.

We do not have the spiritual resources we need for the calling and task of ministry without Christ.

I Don't Have What It Takes

You don't deserve to be a pastor. Even though it was years ago, I can remember him whispering it in my ear as clearly as though it happened a moment ago. In the intervening month between when I accepted the call to serve a church in New Mexico as pastor and when I actually began serving, I heard him say it again and again. When I woke up in the morning, I heard it. When I had spare moments in the day, I heard it. When I laid my head on the pillow at night, I heard it.

You're not qualified. You're a failure. If people knew who you really are, they would never follow you. You don't have what it takes.

The enemy plagued me for a month in a severe time of spiritual attack. I could not understand it, so I called one of my mentors, and we met for lunch. I asked him what I should do. Should I call the church back and tell them I can't come? Are all these things Satan is telling me true?

He gave me some wisdom that I have never forgotten. His advice was simple: "Andrew, when the enemy accuses you, agree with him. Then remind him that it's not about you."

You are not qualified. Yes, you're right. *You're a failure.* Yes, you're right. *If people knew who you really are, they would never follow you.* Yes, you're right. *You don't have what it takes.* Yes, you're right.

But Jesus has what it takes! He is eminently qualified. He's never failed. And when was pastoral ministry about my abilities, my qualifications, my successes, or getting people to follow me?

I need to remind myself frequently that my standing before God and my calling to ministry can never be about my abilities or what I deserve. I'm accepted by God, not based on my own merit, but only because of the merit of Christ. This is the good news of the gospel: Christ does for me what I cannot do for myself.

But that is also good news for ministry. Ministry requires death to myself and my abilities and dependence on the merits of Christ. Paul said, "Therefore, no condemnation now exists for those in Christ Jesus" (Rom. 8:1 HCSB). As long as I am in Christ, I can embrace the accusations of the enemy as accurate and then remind him that although I do not have what it takes, Christ does. On the cross, God judged all of my failures and rebellion by pouring out his wrath on Christ who died on my behalf. Christ's death on the cross means I now stand justified before God, not because I deserve it at all, but because of what Christ has done for me.[3]

The Sufficiency of the Chief Shepherd

I don't have what it takes for ministry. I don't have it all together. I don't have all the answers. But the chief Shepherd does. A truth that will set you free is understanding that you do not have to have what it takes! The great Shepherd of the sheep has everything you need for life and ministry. This is the hope of the pastor: not that you have to be successful or sufficient, but that the One you serve is.

I'll never forget officiating my first funeral. As a twenty-year-old, I had only ever attended a handful of funerals, much less ever thought about conducting one. I had no idea what to do. A woman in the community in which I was pastoring at the time called the church office to ask if I could conduct the funeral even though she wasn't a church member. Of course, I agreed, and I promptly went to her house to visit with her about the service. To my surprise, I discovered that the man who had died was abusive in the home and that his wife was relieved that he had passed. Now how was I supposed to do a funeral for this man? It would have been hard enough to do my first funeral for a faithful Christian. The fact that I was supposed to preach a funeral service for a man about whom I had nothing positive to say made it all the more difficult. It was one of many times I had to acknowledge that I didn't have what it took for the moment. I needed Jesus and his wisdom. The chief Shepherd possessed in that moment what I as the pastor lacked.

That funeral was not as difficult as the first funeral I conducted for a suicide victim. A boy who had not yet reached his teenage years took his life on one of the most tragic days I've ever experienced. The day of his funeral the service was packed with people from the entire community. Several of his young friends spoke during the service. It was more than any pastor could handle. How is a pastor to lead in such a moment? What is he to say? I had to acknowledge again that I didn't have what it took, but Jesus did.

There are so many moments in our ministries where we are faced with an insurmountable challenge, an unbelievable burden, or an impossible situation—the loss of a child, a hurting marriage, a runaway teenager, or a crisis of faith. In those moments, we should not pretend that we have what God's people need. We need to point them to him. More times than I can remember, I have had to come back to God and say, "I can't, but you can. I need you." That's where the spiritual life starts. It is where pastoral life starts. *I need you.*

What you will find in your insufficiency, in your spiritual bankruptcy, is that when you cry out to the all-sufficient Shepherd, he will answer you. Scripture tells us to "approach the throne of grace with boldness, so that we may receive mercy and find grace to help us in time of need" (Heb. 4:16). The Bible assures us that when we cry out for God to do for us what we cannot do for ourselves, he is "a very present help in trouble" (Ps. 46:1 KJV). In fact, this is what the Sermon on the Mount promises.

Ask, Seek, Knock

It's a blessing to come to the realization of our spiritual bankruptcy, but only if that realization presses us into embracing the posture of the next several beatitudes; namely brokenness, humility, and a spiritual thirst for the righteousness of Jesus. You're blessed if you realize that you are spiritually impoverished, but it's not a blessing to stay there. As my friend Shane Pruitt puts it: "It's okay not to be okay, but it's not okay to stay that way!" We all need to move from our spiritual poverty to experience the spiritual riches of Christ.

One evening when my wife and I were dating, I planned to take her to a scenic lookout on Lake Ray Hubbard, just outside of Dallas. On the way to our destination, I pulled off the road and took what I thought was a shortcut through a parking lot. It turned out that the parking lot was a *future* parking lot that at the moment was nothing more than a dirt field. It had rained throughout the day so before we knew it, Amy's car was stuck in the mud. I got out of the car and spent about an hour in my Italian leather shoes and "date night" clothes trying to get the car unstuck, to no avail. We called friends and left the car in the field overnight. The next morning I drove my pickup truck to the future parking lot and tried to get her car pulled out of the mud. This resulted in my truck getting trapped as well. The story gets worse, but I'll cut to the chase. I finally called a friend who had a friend in the local fire department who came out and hooked up both of our vehicles to a fire truck and pulled them out of the mud like a hot knife going through butter. As much as I tried to get unstuck, my problems weren't solved until I called someone with the resources to do something about it.

All of us are spiritually stuck without Christ, and there is nothing we can do to free ourselves. The good news is that if we call on Jesus, he has the resources to move us from spiritual bankruptcy to spiritual fullness. If we cry out to him from the pit of spiritual poverty, the Lord will answer with his riches in Jesus Christ!

This beatitude's thematic counterpart in the Sermon on the Mount is in Matthew 7:7–11.[4] In that passage, Jesus gives a series of repeated commands and promises. "Ask . . . seek . . . knock," Jesus commands. Then he promises, "It will be given to you, . . . you will find, . . . and the door will be opened to you" (v. 7).

The three commands are three ways of saying the same thing: come to God for what you need but don't have. All three commands are present, active, and imperative verbs. The fact that the commands are in the present tense means that the act of asking, seeking, and knocking is not a one-and-done thing. Out of our spiritual poverty we are to be persistent in asking, seeking, and knocking, looking for the Lord to answer us and provide what we don't have. It's continual.

Because the commands are in the active voice, we can know that seeking the Lord in this way is not something that someone else does to or for you. No one can come to

God for you. This is something *you* must do. We are each responsible to ask God for what we need.

That the commands are in the imperative mood means that these are in, indeed, commands. This is not a suggestion or one option of many to take care of our spiritual condition; this is the *only* way, and we are instructed to call out to the Lord in this way.

But notice what glorious promises await those who will ask, seek, and knock. Jesus promises that if you keep asking, it will be given. If you continually seek, you will find. If you go on knocking, the door will be opened. This is an assurance from Jesus that if you are spiritually bankrupt and you want the riches of Christ for your spiritual need, he *will* give it to you.

Jesus uses an analogy in verses 9–11 of a father who is asked for something by a child. He says that in the same way that a human father gives his children what they need, God knows how to give good gifts to those who ask him. I have four children. Sometimes my kids will wake me up early on Saturday mornings and ask, "Daddy, can we watch cartoons?" If they wake me up to ask, my immediate answer is not usually yes. But my youngest daughter knows how to ask the question in such a way as to get the answer she wants. She's learned to ask, "Daddy, will you come watch cartoons with me?" I can't say no to that. Who could resist a cute three-year-old asking to snuggle with dad and watch Saturday-morning cartoons? The truth is, I'm eager to say yes. I want good gifts for my children.

Pastor, here's the truth: we don't have what it takes spiritually—not in salvation, not in sanctification, not even in pastoral ministry. But God is a loving Father who is eager to give good gifts to his children. And when someone recognizes their spiritual inability, God longs to show his ability in their lives. If we will take our eyes off our poverty and place our sight on Jesus, God will answer and give us what we need for our lives and our ministries.

Are you spiritually stuck? Call out to Jesus. Do you face an insurmountable obstacle in your ministry leadership? Call out to Jesus. Are you discouraged and depressed in your place of ministry? Call out to Jesus. Are you embarrassed that your life and your family are in broken pieces even as you try to piece other lives together? Call out to Jesus. Do you need something you don't currently have but that he does? Call out to Jesus.

Jesus is eager to fill you up with what you lack. Isn't that good news?

Pastor, You Need the Gospel, Too

— Nathan Lorick —

Gospel-centered ministry seems to be on the rise. Everywhere you turn in the evangelical world, you hear about a church, a ministry, or a Christian leader being "gospel centered." This is something to celebrate. The gospel is and should be the "main thing" in the church. As pastors, we base our lives and callings on it.

Yet, if we aren't careful, the gospel can become more of a buzzword than the powerful change agent it is. The term gospel *is more than merely a ministry catchphrase or a catalyst for a sermon series. It's easy to use the word so often that we forget why the gospel is so important in the first place and why we need to embrace it.*

When I was a pastor, I knew how important it was to share the gospel personally and in my sermons. I knew the gospel was "the power of God for salvation to everyone who believes" (Rom. 1:16). My clever series title or expository sermon could only go so far, so I was diligent to incorporate the gospel into every message. The gospel should always be central.

However, for many years I thought the gospel was important only for unbelievers. I operated without the truth that, as a follower of Christ and as a pastor, I needed the gospel too. A breakthrough moment came for me a few years ago, when I realized that the gospel is not something you encounter once and then move past. The gospel is meant to be encountered daily. Allow me to share three reasons this is true in the life of a pastor.

First, we are broken. It's true. You and I are broken individuals. We never graduate from the gospel because we never graduate from our brokenness. This is why we need the gospel daily. Life has a way of bringing you face-to-face with your humanity. In the inner depths of your heart, your humanity screams, "I am broken." This is not a bad thing, thanks to the gospel. Our brokenness is not a setback; it is a setup. God uses our brokenness in his sovereign plan. My brokenness drives me to the gospel as a daily remedy. After all, the greatest leaders in the Bible walked with a spiritual limp. The gospel reminds me of my desperate need for the goodness and graciousness of God every single day.

Second, our gifts are limited. There are so many gifted pastors and leaders across the landscape of ministry. I envy some pastors' ability to communicate and lead. The world certainly does not lack for gifted ministers. However, the hard truth is that our giftedness only goes so far without the power of the gospel. Psalm 4:3 reminds us that God desires our godliness, not our gifts. The psalmist declares: "Know that the LORD has set apart the faithful for himself." It's not our impressiveness that sets us apart. It is our pursuit of God that sets us apart, which is only possible through the gospel. The calling the Lord has given us is not fueled by creativity, innovation, or ability. Our calling is fueled by the gospel. The power is not in anything we do but, rather, what God has already done through the gospel. As pastors, we desperately need the gospel daily to rescue us from the lie that we can depend on our own abilities. When our securities are more rooted in what we can accomplish rather than what he has accomplished, our ministries are in danger. God will do more with a surrendered heart than an impressive ability.

Third, life and ministry are messy. Being a pastor is the greatest calling and the worst job in the world. It's the greatest calling because you get to partner with God on the front lines of pushing back darkness and seeing lives changed. It's the worst job because of the strain of ministry. Paul shows us this in 2 Corinthians 11:28 when he says, "Not to mention other things, there is the daily pressure on me: my concern for all the churches." Ministry is hard. The calling to pastor is hard. This is exactly why pastors need the gospel too. God uses the gospel to bring order out of chaos and to turn a mess into a message. He takes even the most difficult circumstances of our lives and uses them for his purposes.

Pastor, you need the gospel too. You are called, equipped, faithful, gifted, and being used by God. Let us remember daily, the gospel is not a one-time encounter; it is a daily gift from God himself.

CHAPTER 4

The Broken Pastor

"Blessed are those who mourn, for they will be comforted."

—Matthew 5:4

On October 19, 1856, Charles Spurgeon was preaching to an overflow crowd of several thousand people at the Surrey Garden Music Hall in London when he experienced perhaps the greatest tragedy of his life. As thousands crowded into the building with thousands more waiting outside, someone shouted that there was a fire and the balconies were collapsing. One of the balconies did indeed collapse, and the crowd started stampeding to get out of the building. In the chaos, several people were trampled, and before it was all over, seven people were killed and twenty-eight injured.

The effect of this calamity on Spurgeon's heart and life was profound. He suffered from depression and carried around a sadness that never left him until he died. Spurgeon understood mourning. Yet God used this tragedy in Spurgeon's life and ministry to push him toward Christ. In fact, Spurgeon would later say, "I have learned to kiss the wave that throws me against the Rock of Ages."[1]

The waves that bring mourning are hard to bear, but we can learn to kiss the waves if we will see that they push us toward Christ. The second beatitude calls us to a posture we should embrace once we understand the meaning of the first beatitude. When we come to realize our spiritual unworth before God, it should lead us to deep mourning and brokenness over our sin.

Jesus teaches us that those who "mourn" are blessed (Matt. 5:4). This is not Jesus asking his followers to constantly mope about with long faces. Mourning is not moping. No, Christianity is a joyful faith. This mourning comes on the heels of recognizing our spiritual poverty. When we come face-to-face with the reality of our own sin, the result should be a deep mourning over our sin. The word translated "mourn" in most major Bible translations means to be "grieved," "sad," or "broken" over our sin. William Barclay suggests the meaning of verse 4 as follows: "Blessed is the man who is desperately sorry for his own sin and his own unworthiness."[2] Indeed, Kent Hughes reminds us: "No one is truly a Christian who has not mourned over his or her sins."[3]

Broken over Our Sin

When I pastored in New Mexico, we lived in a pretty desolate part of the Permian Basin region of southeast New Mexico and West Texas. We had a sweet couple in our church who would invite us over to their home from time to time in the evenings. Their backyard was an oasis in the desert. Mrs. Stone filled her backyard with all kinds of plants and flowers. I still don't know how she kept them alive in the desert. One of her unique gifts was the ability to craft beautiful pieces of pottery that she would place among the plants in the backyard garden. Her particular way of forming her pottery pieces was to take a piece of pottery, break it into many pieces, and then reshape the pieces into something beautiful. Like the beautiful mosaic floors in many European cathedrals and bathhouses, Mrs. Stone's pottery made something beautiful out of that which was broken.

God loves working among the broken things of life. Broken lives are ripe for God's healing hand. "The LORD is near the brokenhearted," Psalm 34:18 teaches us. I wonder if the reason so many churches are missing a sense of God's presence is because of the presence of great pride rather than great grief over our sin. How many of us describe our churches as broken over sin? Maybe the reason we don't sense the nearness of the Lord is because we lack brokenness over our sin.

So often, pastors are ready to (humble)brag about their church's stats like they are reading the back of a baseball card. We celebrate numbers—how many are in attendance, how large our budget is, or how many people watched our services online. We revel in the big, the bold, and the beautiful. But brokenness? I hardly think most of our churches could be accused of being too grieved over our sin. Maybe that's because our churches are led by pastors who aren't broken enough over their own sin. We have many bold pastors—bold in the truth, bold in their preaching, bold about their gifts and abilities. But how many of us could be described as broken? Remember that Paul came to the Corinthian church not in power, but in weakness (1 Cor. 2:3).

Let me confess something. One of the indications I've seen in my own life when I'm distant from the Lord is that I have a hard time specifically identifying my sin, other than in pretty generic ways. One indication that we are growing closer to the Lord is that we are more, not less, aware of our sin.

How can you tell if you are broken over your sin? First, we should be able to identify specific sins against the Lord. Second, once it has been identified, rather than minimizing or glossing over that sin, we must name it, confess it, and grieve over it. Only when our sin has been recognized and grieved can we say that we are genuinely broken over it. Our churches will never be broken before the Lord until we have broken pastors who see personal sin as grievous as it really is.

Many of our church members would be shocked if they knew their pastor also struggles with sin. That shouldn't be shocking. Pastors are people too. Pastors aren't perfect and don't have it all together. God forbid that we pretend otherwise. We need the posture of the publican who said, "God, have mercy on me, a sinner," rather than the Pharisee who self-righteously and self-deceptively said, "God, I thank you that I'm not like other people" (Luke 18:10–13). There is comfort available for mourners, but there is no comfort without first mourning.

As pastors, we are pretty good about leading the church in vision, in strategy, in exciting new endeavors, but more important than any of those things is that we lead in brokenness over our sin. We should be the first to recognize our sin, the first to confess, and the first to repent. We cannot properly grieve over anyone else's sin until we have first grieved over our own.

Mourning over the Sin of the World

The church needs pastors who are broken over personal sin. But we also need pastors who grieve over the sin that wrecks others. We can't passionately proclaim the hope of Christ until we are fed up with how sin destroys individual lives, homes, marriages, cities, and even nations.

Three times in the Gospels, Jesus spit as part of a healing miracle (Mark 7:31–37; 8:23; John 9:6). I had never really thought about why Jesus did this until I heard a pastor suggest that this would have been a signal of disgust in the ancient world. It may be that in this act Jesus was visually and viscerally displaying his disgust at sin's effects in the lives of the people he came to redeem. This isn't the only time Jesus is visibly affected by sin's effects.

At the tomb of Lazarus, John tells us simply, "Jesus wept" (John 11:35). Jesus was as touched by death as we are and more so. Matthew's Gospel uses a vivid term, normally translated "compassion" but conveying a gut-level depth of feeling, to describe Jesus' reaction when he saw the crowd "like sheep without a shepherd" (Matt. 9:36). As he approached the city of Jerusalem and surveyed it, Jesus again wept (Luke 19:41). As he entered the temple and observed how people were being taken advantage of and being excluded by others, he was moved with just wrath and began throwing the money changers out of the temple (Luke 19:45–46). In these instances and others, we see that Jesus was moved deeply by how he saw sin at work in the world and, more immediately, in the people around him.

I think the first time I consciously remember hating what sin was doing in the world was when I was a kid and my first dog died. I remember putting my dog in a little grave in the backyard and just weeping. I hated death so much in that moment. That hatred for sin and death has only intensified in the years since. In every cancer diagnosis, at the announcement of every divorce, in funeral after funeral I sense it again, a deep mourning over what sin does not only in me, but in those around me.

The example of our chief Shepherd shows us that pastors must not only mourn over personal sin, but we also must be grieved over the sin of the world. We must hate sin if we are to turn from it in our own lives and serve as agents of God's rescue in the lives of those to whom we minister, saving others "by snatching them from the fire" (Jude 23). In fact, I do not think it's possible for any of us to do our jobs rightly as pastors without this deep personal grief over sin and its effects. The Puritan Thomas Watson said, "Till sin be bitter, Christ will not be sweet."⁴ Do you sufficiently mourn over the plague of sin that harms us and the world in which we serve?

The Whole of the Christian Life is Repentance

What is the aim of this brokenness over personal and corporate sin? The apostle Paul tells us what brokenness over sin should produce: "For godly grief produces a repentance that leads to salvation without regret, but worldly grief produces death" (2 Cor. 7:10). A broken pastor is a repentant pastor. Brokenness unaccompanied by repentance is not true brokenness. Those who mourn are blessed and comforted, but only if mourning is the grief that produces a turning from sin.

At the All Saints' Church in Wittenberg, Germany, stand two commemorative bronze doors weighing twenty-two hundred pounds. Inscribed on the doors is a duplication of the text of the Ninety-five Theses originally nailed to the door by the great Protestant Reformer Martin Luther on October 31, 1517. Luther's first thesis states: "When our Lord and Master Jesus Christ said, 'Repent'

(Matt. 4:17), he willed the entire life of believers to be one of repentance." In other words, repentance isn't just important as a one-time act in justification; it is a day-by-day expectation in the process of sanctification. As a believer and a pastor, I am called to a life of repentance.

Pastor, repentance should be an everyday act in your life as you continually confront and mourn over sin in your life. Repentance is where mourning leads us. A repentant life is a blessed life. Blessed are those who mourn.

Satan would love nothing more than to use our sin to neutralize us and our ministry. He wants us to wallow in it, to return to it, to feel guilt over it. The one thing Satan does not want is for us to mourn over it, because when we mourn and repent, God repairs what is broken.

When we are broken over sin, God can begin to rebuild our lives. My wife and I try to exercise on a regular basis. When you exercise a muscle, the tissue in that muscle actually tears. Gym rats are sometimes referred to as "ripped," but that is literally what is happening when we work out—the muscle is breaking down. But as the muscle tissue begins to repair, it is rebuilt stronger than it was before. Brokenness leads to rebuilding. As believers and as pastors, God can use our brokenness if it leads to repentance. He can take broken pieces and rebuild them into something beautiful.

I do not know how life, ministry, or your sin may have broken you. Sometimes we mourn over what we have done. Sometimes we mourn over what has been done to us. Perhaps you've experienced a church hurt. Maybe you're struggling in your marriage or your parenting. Or perhaps a struggle with a personal sin is leaving you battered and bruised. In our broken moments it's easy to ask: "Why, God?" We wonder why God is allowing this particular experience into our lives that causes such deep sorrow. A more difficult but much more fruitful question to ask is: "God, what are you trying to do in me through this?" When you ask that question, God will begin to show you what he is trying to build into your life in the midst of what sin has broken. God can redeem these broken places in our lives. As he redeems those moments of mourning, he can also begin to use our lives to mend brokenness in others as well. John Claypool once described the "secret of ministry" as consisting of two things: "First, the faithful tending of one's own woundedness, and second, the willingness to move to the aid of another and make the fruits of one's own woundedness available to others."[5]

Something Better to Offer

The church and the world need pastors who hate sin and sin's effects, who are truly sick of what this world has to offer, and who model a life of repentance. Only when we are fed up with sin and faithful in repentance can we begin to offer something better to the world. But we have nothing better to offer anyone else until we have first walked the path of brokenness ourselves.

The third beatitude's chiastic counterpart in the Sermon on the Mount is found in Matthew 7:1–6.[6] The first of these verses probably rivals John 3:16 as the most well-known verse in the Bible: "Do not judge, so that you won't be judged." It is also one of the most misunderstood verses in the Bible. At first, it appears to be a blanket prohibition of judging others. It is accompanied by a warning that we will be judged according to the same standard with which we judge others (v. 2). Jesus asks a piercing question: "Why do you look at the splinter in your brother's eye but don't notice the beam of wood in your own eye?" (v. 3). This is an alarming question. Jesus is indicating that we may do more harm than good if we try to fix what is broken in others before Jesus fixes what is broken in us.

I heard a story a number of years ago about a single mom in an urban city who heard a large crash in her home in the middle of the night. Suspecting a burglar might be in the house, she grabbed her shotgun and started walking through the house. When she got to the kitchen and turned on the light, she heard a noise behind her. She whirled around with her gun to see who it was. Her heart stopped as she realized that the crash in the house was caused by her young daughter who had gotten up to get a drink, her daughter at whom the shotgun was now pointed. In her hurry to confront what she thought was a danger in her home, this mother unwittingly became the most dangerous person in the room.

Many Christians (and pastors!) look at the sin they see in those around them and are quick to address it. We know how dangerous sin can be. But if we rush to confront sin in others before we confront the sin in us, we actually become as dangerous as the sin we are confronting.

What's surprising about the verses to follow is that Jesus actually seems to say the opposite of what most people believe these verses mean. In verse 5, Jesus instructs us to take the beam of wood out of our eye first so that we can then see clearly to take the splinter out of our brother's eye. Jesus is not saying in this section that we are not to judge the world. No. In fact, Paul says, "Don't you know that the saints will judge the world?" (1 Cor. 6:2). Jesus is saying that we should not go about looking for specks in others' eyes *before* addressing the beams of sin in our own. Jesus is calling out our hypocrisy in these verses. We cannot do anything about the sin in others until we have first dealt with our own sin, and it is the worst kind of hypocrisy to go around pointing out the sins of people "out there" when we haven't first dealt with the sin in us.

As ambassadors of Christ who extend the message of reconciliation to the world (2 Cor. 5:19–20), our chief Shepherd has commissioned us to call the world to something better than the sin that wreaks havoc on their lives. We must draw people's attention to how their sin is causing ruin and misery. But until we are first broken over our own sin and realize that we need repentance as much as our sheep, we dangerously wield weapons that harm those around us. We have nothing to offer the world that's better than their sin until we are first sick of our own sin and have tasted of God's comfort as we turn to him in repentance. Once we have drunk deeply of God's grace in our mourning over sin, we have something we can offer the flock. As John Claypool said, "We will make our greatest impact in preaching when we dare to make available to the woundedness of others what we have learned through an honest grappling with our own woundedness."[7]

Repentance Is for the Redeemed

– Robert Smith Jr. –

I once heard of a man who had great power and influence, but he had committed great sin and was apparently unrepentant of it. He went to see his religious leader who would eventually become the highest ranking official in their denomination. The religious leader took him to a fountain filled with rocks that had been submerged under the flowing water for many years. The leader lifted a rock from the fountain and broke it in half. The rock had been in the water, but the water had never been in the rock. It was wet on the outside and dry on the inside.

My fellow pastors, we need to remember the postulation of Martin Luther, the sixteenth-century Protestant Reformer: "We, the redeemed, are in a state of simul justus et pecator [simultaneously saint and sinner]." We need to continually repent after we have been redeemed! We have been justified, we are being sanctified, and we will be glorified. We are the redeemed. And yet the redeemed need to live in a state of continuous repentance.

John Wesley, the father of Methodism, stressed what he considered were the grand doctrines of Methodism:

1. Repentance, *which he referred to as "the porch of religion;"*
2. Justification, *which he called "the door of religion;" and*
3. Sanctification, *which he understood to be "religion itself."*

We need to return to the porch of repentance. Justification is a past act of God. Sanctification is a present, progressive work of God. Glorification is God's eschatological reality for us for the future. We must hear our Lord's admonition to the church in Ephesus: "Repent, and do the works you did at first" (Rev. 2:5).

What is pastoral repentance? We know what repentance is for the unredeemed. We have inscribed on the canvas of our minds the picture of the Pentecostal scene of Jews gathered in Jerusalem for the Feast of Pentecost. Upon hearing the gospel in their own language, they were convicted of their sins and "pierced to the heart." They asked Peter and the rest of the apostles, "What should we do?" The first thing Peter responded was, "Repent!" Approximately three thousand Jews repented and were redeemed (Acts 2:37–41).

As pastors, we repent because we are saved. We want to be maximally used by God and do not want to settle for a ministry of mediocrity. Only when the curtain of eternity is rolled back in the eschaton will we know for certain what we could have done and where we could have been in ministry if we had kept the way clear and let nothing come between our soul and our Savior. Do we love our sin more than we love our Savior?

I remember reading "The Shepherd," a sermon by the sixteenth-century Protestant Reformer Huldrych Zwingli, who recommended that pastors should begin to preach as Christ began: "'Repent!'" He believed, "No one will repent who does not know how evil he is. . . . Illness must always be recognized before one takes the medicine. Here the gospel and repentance are connected; for no one really rejoices in the gospel who has not previously rightly recognized the disease of sin."[1]

Repentance is a change of heart and/or direction. Repentance is for the redeemed—even pastors—and not just unredeemed sinners! In the first of his Ninety-five Theses, Martin Luther described repentance as: "When our Lord and Master Jesus Christ said, 'Repent' (Matt. 4:17), he meant that the entire life of believers be a life of repentance."[2]

As a young pastor, I remember preparing to leave my house on a Sunday morning to go preach to my congregation. The sermon title was "The Greatest Love Story Ever Told." The sermon was based on Hosea and anticipated the love of God in Christ. I felt good about the sermon. I had spent many hours studying and preparing to preach it. I was ready—at least I thought I was. There was only one problem: I caused a presermonic "domestic discussion" with my wife moments before we left the house to go to church. My temperament was terrible and my attitude was wrong. Yet I was on my way to church to preach "The Greatest Love Story Ever Told!" Before I could preach on love, I had to repent to God and apologize to my wife. I have had the privilege of preaching the gospel nearly fifty-four years. I consider the sermon I preached after my repentance to God and apology to my wife as one of the most powerful moments in which God, by his grace, chose to use me.

CHAPTER 5

The Humble Pastor

"Blessed are the humble, for they will inherit the earth."

—Matthew 5:5

On an almost weekly basis, I get an email from another ministry consulting firm offering to help me develop and elevate my "brand," multiply my platform, expand my reach as a thought leader, become an influencer, cultivate my image, or other such nonsensical hogwash—all for a fee, of course. I am often tempted to reply with: "You are doing it wrong!" It is sad to say, but "brand" management and image development are all the rage right now among pastors. It's all about platform, influence, "reach," and ultimately, renown.

There is a saying in West Texas: "I ride for the brand." Cowhands use the word *brand* almost in the exact opposite sense as "brand developers" use it. This phrase means that

it's not about you, but whom you serve. It is about loyalty
to the ranch and the rancher. I find this to be a much more
biblical approach than many of the influence peddlers who
clog up my email in-box. In pastoral ministry, as in the
Christian life, it is not about you. As a friend of mine says,
"When pride walks onto the platform, God walks off."
Blessed are the humble.

I recently heard a refreshing sermon. On August 20,
2019, Jamie Dew delivered his inaugural address as president of New Orleans Baptist Theological Seminary.[1] He
used a couple of unforgettable metaphors to frame the
nature of church work and our ministry calling. He called
future pastors to take up "the towel and the basin." That is
a fitting metaphor for ministry! The towel and the basin
refer to the tools you need to wash feet. Foot washing isn't
glamorous. It is not a highly sought-after vocation. It is the
job of a servant. It's the job of a pastor. Pastors are called
to the towel and the basin. We are called to pour ourselves
out for the flock in humility. What a far cry from the posture many of us want to take. Dew concluded his message
by saying, "There's a little bit of peacock in each of us."

Ah, the peacock. A bird that loves to fluff its feathers
and strut its stuff. Pastoral peacocks love to do the same
thing. It's easier to do than we probably want to admit.
Pastoral ministry is a public job. In some communities,
the pastor of the church takes on almost mayoral qualities. He's invited to this event and that ceremony, and his
presence is usually acknowledged and applauded. A lot
of attention is paid to the pastor in these environments.

It goes with the territory. But that doesn't mean we have to *enjoy* it. If the recognition and applause draw an inner smile, we are in peacock territory.

Every year a pastoral intern comes and serves with me for the summer to get a taste of what pastoral ministry is like. The first assignment on the first day for my interns is to clean every restroom in the basement of our main building (nearly a dozen toilets!). It's quite an introduction to ministry. It's an accurate introduction. I don't want an intern to walk into our church and see the large buildings, the many people, the sizable budget, and the comfortable pastor's study and get in their minds that this is what ministry is all about. I want them to understand that ministry happens on our knees as we serve others. I remind them that a large church isn't normative. Most churches are no more than 250 people, which means the pastor wears many hats, and few of them are glamorous. In my first couple of pastorates I wore the hats of preacher, janitor, lawn mower, occasional music leader, and many other responsibilities seminary didn't prepare me for. But that's what ministry is about—humble service of Jesus and his people.

As pastors, we are servants, not masters. We are shepherds, not kings. We should not occupy ourselves with concerns about brand, platform, influence, or thought leadership (whatever that is). Our calling is higher and holier than that. We are pastors entrusted with the care of sheep. That's a hard, gritty, smelly task. It's one that requires humility.

Hubris and Humility

Perhaps the virtue of humility can be most clearly understood by considering its opposite vice, hubris. Hubris was the Greek goddess of prideful arrogance. Hubris was a spirit that could be fostered by anyone at any point in time, causing them to act recklessly and take unnecessary risks due to their prideful self-appraisal. Hubris was seen in the life (and death) of Icarus, the Greek god who was banished to the island of Crete with his father, Daedalus. Attempting to escape, his father, a master craftsman, constructed wings for them both out of feathers and wax. As they began to fly away from the island, Daedalus warned Icarus of hubris and told him not to fly too close to the sun lest his wings should melt. Icarus ignored his father's advice, flew too close to the sun, and as his wings began to melt, he fell out of the sky and drowned in the sea. To this day, the Icarian Sea in the Mediterranean stands as a reminder to beware the hubris of Icarus. Indeed, any one of us is in danger of flying too close to the sun, going beyond our limits because we simply don't recognize them.

Icarus's mistake was going a step too far, going beyond his limits, thinking he couldn't fall no matter how close to danger he flew. In an unusual verse that shows us that hubris affects more than just men, Jude tells us of an angelic rebellion where "angels . . . did not keep their own position but abandoned their proper dwelling" (Jude 6). That's what hubris is. It is going beyond the boundaries God has for us until we make a wreck of our lives.

The biblical embodiment of hubris is Nebuchadnezzar. The king of Babylon was a madman whose hubris drove him to construct a nine-story statue of himself and order everyone under his rule to bow in worship to it under pain of death. His egomania came and went throughout his life. At one point he looked over his kingdom and declared: "Is this not Babylon the Great *that I have built* to be a royal residence *by my vast power and for my majestic glory?*" (Dan. 4:30, emphasis added). This drove him from the palace to the pasture, where he lived like a wild animal and ate grass until he acknowledged "that the Most High is ruler over human kingdoms" (v. 32). His sin was taking a step too far, going beyond the boundaries God had placed for him.

Few people in history have epitomized the vice of prideful hubris more than Nebuchadnezzar. A close runner-up is Napoleon. Napoleon had once-in-a-millennium leadership giftings. He had a meteoric rise to leadership in the midst of the French Revolution, becoming a general at the tender age of twenty-four. He was a military genius who won fifty-three of the sixty battles he fought. As an omen of things to come, when Napoleon was coronated at Notre Dame Cathedral, he placed the imperial crown over his own head while the Pope stood by and watched, a vivid picture of what Napoleon thought of himself—the ultimate "self-made" man.[2]

Like Nebuchadnezzar, Napoleon saw himself as an invincible emperor. But like Icarus, Napoleon's mistake was going a step too far, going beyond his limits, assuming he could not be defeated. His pride led him to one of the most stunning military losses in history at the Battle of Waterloo, ending his rule as emperor of France. Napoleon's remains now sit above the city of Paris in the chapel at the Dôme de Invalides with an inscription on his tomb stating his desire to be buried "among the people of France who loved me so much." Like Nebuchadnezzar, Napoleon's legacy is that of a self-infatuated leader who sought glory for himself but finished with a whimper.

We find quite the contrast with the portrait of Jesus given to us by the apostle Paul in Philippians 2. Paul says in verses 5–8:

> Adopt the same attitude as that of Christ Jesus, who, existing in the form of God, did not consider equality with God as something to be exploited. Instead he emptied himself by assuming the form of a servant, taking on the likeness of humanity. And when he had come as a man, he humbled himself by becoming obedient to the point of death—even to death on a cross.

Jesus modeled humility. Even though he was God himself, he emptied himself of his divine right and embraced the posture of a servant who would be humbled in pouring himself out for us on the cross. Jesus showed his disciples what humility looked like when he took the towel and the basin in John 13 and washed his disciples' feet. He not only explained what humility looked like; he clearly expected it from those who would lead the church, telling his disciples not to use their position to "lord it over" those who would follow them but, rather, to become great by embracing servanthood (Mark 10:42–45). True greatness is not found in exploiting your position over others, but in emptying yourself for others. That's the essence of humility. C. S. Lewis once said that the truly humble man will not be obsessing about humility. Rather, "he won't be thinking about himself at all."[3] Or as Eugene Peterson put it: "You are at your pastoral best when you are not noticed."[4] The humble pastor will prioritize Christ and Christ's people above himself and his ego.

Would you say your heart is more defined by hubris or humility? Are you content within the boundaries God has placed for you, or are you characterized by self-infatuation and the need for attention from others? Or to put it like the prophet Jeremiah put it: "Do you pursue great things for yourself? Stop pursuing!" (Jer. 45:5).

Pastor, be careful about pursuing great things for yourself. If you are infatuated with self, you are not infatuated with Christ. Our hubris can be masked so easily in seemingly righteous pursuits. We often clothe our hunger for platform or increased social media influence with our desire to get the message of Christ out to as many people as possible. It is a subtle temptation to swap out Christ's renown for our own. The danger, as Kevin Vanhoozer has put it, is "the temptation for pastors to view themselves as the heroes of their own story."[5]

Paul gives us a helpful reminder in Romans 12:3: "I tell everyone among you not to think of himself more highly than he should think." It is easy in ministry to think great and glorious thoughts for ourselves. It's easy to go to pastors' conferences and (humble)brag about how well our church is doing or the great things we appear to be accomplishing. So much energy is devoted among pastors to cultivating and sustaining our image as a "successful" pastor. But brothers, the only image we need to cultivate is the image of Christ.

Humility and Glory

Jesus said those who are humble are blessed (Matt. 5:5). Humble pastors are blessed. I think if we were honest though, some of us would admit that we fear some of the implications of humility. *If I don't promote myself, how will I get ahead? How will I be noticed? How will I be known? How will I get the call to go lead the big church?* But Jesus has good news for these concerns.

The third beatitude's thematic counterpart in the Sermon on the Mount is found in Matthew 6:19–34, where Jesus addresses the potential worries we can experience in life.[6] In verse 25, he says, "Don't worry about your life." He repeats that command in verse 31 and again in verse 34. The reason he gives for this command is liberating. He invites us to consider how God provides for the birds of the air and the flowers of the field. He asks in verse 26:

"Aren't you worth more than they?" In verse 30, he asks: "Won't he do much more for you?" Think about that. The God of the universe, who takes care of everything he created, looks at you and me and says we are *worth* something and he will do more for us than he does for other creatures he has made. Just as freeing as that thought is what Jesus says next. In verse 32, Jesus tells us we don't need to worry about our material needs because "your heavenly Father knows that you need them."

If you are worried that by assuming a posture of humility, no one will recognize or care about you, here's great news: you *are* known, you *are* noticed, and the God who knows and notices will provide everything you truly need. Remember, those who are humble are blessed, "for they will inherit the earth" (Matt. 5:5). Those who realize they have nothing are in a position to receive everything God has to give. Truly, our heavenly Father knows what we need. He gives us more than we even know we need. What he gives the humble is nothing short of glory itself.

There is an important element of Paul's theology in the early part of Romans. In Romans 3:23, he says that "all have sinned and fall short of the glory of God." In our sin, there is no participation in God's glory. But there is a glorious shift in Romans 5:1. Paul says that because we have been declared righteous through faith in Christ and what he has done on our behalf, we enjoy several benefits. For instance, he says that we have peace with God and access to God. One of the benefits he lists often goes unnoticed, but it is so important. In verse 2, Paul says, "We boast in the hope of the glory of God." Scholars note that this could mean that Paul's hope is centered in the glory God has in himself. Others suggest that Paul is saying that his hope is in the glory *which comes from* God. If that's true, then Romans 5:2 is the reversal of Romans 3:23. Without Christ, we fall hopelessly short of God's glory. But in Christ, we will be *clothed* with God's glory! Paul states that point just a few chapters later when he says that we will be "glorified" (Rom. 8:30).

What does it mean to share in the glory of God? C. S. Lewis explores that exact question in his classic essay, "The Weight of Glory." Lewis says that what first comes to mind when he thinks of the concept of glory is either the sense of being famous or of being luminous, of recognition or of radiance. Actually, recognition and radiance are exactly what is entailed in participating in God's glory. Lewis brilliantly explains that glory doesn't mean fame with people or being radiant or bright like a light bulb. Instead, to participate in God's glory means to have "fame with God, approval . . . by God."[7] It has the sense of being "noticed by God."[8] It means that, in Christ, God looks you over and approves of you. He recognizes and favors you. What a glorious thought! But beyond that, he also clothes us with radiance. Lewis continues by considering "the other sense of glory—glory as brightness, splendor, luminosity." He says, "We are to shine as the sun, we are to be given the Morning Star." We will see the beauty of God and "be united with the beauty we see, to pass into it, to receive it into ourselves, to bathe in it, to become part of it."⁹ We will share in the radiant beauty of God as he clothes us with glory.

We will be radiant. We will be recognized. That's what it means to "boast in the hope of the glory of God" (Rom. 5:2).

Here's why that matters: If we are noticed by or "famous with" God, it eliminates our need for status, position, pride, or recognition by others. We have all the recognition we need in Christ. Being favored by God and covered in his beauty is the highest status and position we can ever have. What else could we want?

When Saul was converted, he came to understand this change from being recognized by others to being recognized by God. It was such a big shift for Saul that God changed his name to *Paul*, which means "humble." Saul became "small." When Jesus took hold of Paul's life, he went from "a Hebrew of Hebrews" (Phil. 3:5 NASB) to someone who consistently described himself in the humblest term possible, as a "bond-servant" (Rom. 1:1 NASB). He said that he considered all of his earthly reasons for boasting to be nothing in comparison to the surpassing worth of knowing Christ (Phil. 3:7–8). He understood God's economy: "God has chosen what is insignificant and despised in the world—what is viewed as nothing—to bring to nothing what is viewed as something" (1 Cor. 1:28). God's kingdom is often upside down and backward to our way of thinking. A prideful spirit comes before a fall (Prov. 16:18). The humble inherit the earth (Matt. 5:5).

God will "bring down the tall tree, and make the low tree tall" (Ezek. 17:24).

Kill the Peacock

When I struggle with pride, it's helpful to remember why I'm in ministry in the first place. I'm not in ministry for me. One of my life verses is Romans 11:36 which says, "For from him and through him and *to* him are all things" (emphasis added). Paul says it similarly in Colossians 1:16: "All things have been created through him and *for* him" (emphasis added). All things are *for* him. My life is *for* him. My ministry is *for* him. My preaching is *for* him. My church is *for* him. Jesus is our *telos*—he is the purpose for our lives and ministries and the goal toward which it is all heading. It's all about him. It's not about me. The moment my ministry is about me, it's not about him.

Let's face it. Ministry is a minefield for pride. We are all in danger of hero worship in our churches, networks, or denominations. This will land your ministry dead on arrival. There's no room for ego in the pastorate. Ego is a blessing killer. Kill your ego, or your ego will kill your ministry. There's one hero in ministry, and his name is Jesus.

Jamie Dew concluded his inaugural message at New Orleans Seminary with a simple exhortation: "Kill the peacock." There *is* a little bit of peacock in each one of us. A prideful spirit must be put to death, or it will be the death of a God-blessed ministry. Blessed are the humble.

Humility in the Life of the Pastor

– Doug Munton –

"I need God." Read those three simple words again. They can keep you and your ministry from harm and heartbreak and waste.

There are many ways to mess up in ministry—sexual immorality, improper use of money, and unresolved anger come to mind. But a more insidious enemy has undermined many pastors. It can go almost unnoticed and frequently unchallenged. The great enemy of pride will slay any ministry leader who leaves it unchecked. And, unfortunately, I've seen its awful toll taken on many talented young ministers over the years.

Notice the Bible's warning about the danger of pride: "Pride comes before destruction, and an arrogant spirit before a fall" (Prov. 16:18). These are strong words of warning for any willing to hear.

Humility is the opposite of pride. It is your recognition of your deep need for God. It is your understanding of your inherent weakness and God's available strength. It reminds you that you can't face life and ministry successfully in your own power and through your own talents.

When we are humble, we depend on God instead of our-selves. When pride takes over, we trust our abilities, talents, and gifts.

Let me suggest two understandings that will aid you in your desire to live a life of humility rather than pride. Knowing and living these truths can keep you from the dangers that come with pride and lead you to the God-honoring life that comes from humility.

First, recognize the limits of your abilities. I know you have talents, gifts, and abilities. God knows these things as well. After all, they come from him. But you also need to know your limitations, weaknesses, and blind spots.

While you affirm that you need the Lord, pride whispers in your ear, "But you don't need him that much." Pride suggests that you are pretty talented and that God is actually fortunate to have someone of your caliber on his side! Humility knows you are gifted by God. But it also knows the limitations of those gifts.

Please don't forget the truth of who you are. You are a sinner saved by grace, not by merit (Eph. 1:8). You tend to stray from God like sheep from the shepherd. You are incapable of knowing the twists and turns of the future, and you struggle just to make sense of the present. You tend to give yourself the benefit of the doubt and to ignore your shortcomings. All of these things are true about you and all mankind. Humility is the result of your recognition of these truths.

Knowing your limits is key to usefulness in ministry. It is the key to strength, power, and victory.

Second, learn to trust God's unlimited ability to use you.
Humility teaches you that you are limited, but God is unlim-
ited. It teaches you that you are weak, but God is strong. It tells
you not to depend upon yourself, but upon God's ability to use
someone like you.

The danger with the talented and the gifted is that they
can settle for their limited abilities instead of tapping into God's
unlimited abilities. Nothing personal, but God is much smarter
than you!

God wants to use you in his work. He calls frail, fallen
people like you into his service all the time. In fact, those are the
only kind of people he has. So trust God to use you. Ministry
isn't dependent on your abilities, but His.

When you begin to depend on God and not yourself, you
will find he is absolutely dependable. You will find a greater
desire to know the truth and wisdom of his word. You will dis-
cover new joy in talking to him in prayer. And your service will
take on deeper meaning as you begin to join him in the work he
already has prepared for you to do.

Do you remember those three simple words I started with?
Keep those words close to your life and near to your heart. Be
honest with yourself and with the Lord. Fight against pride
and arrogance and walk in the path of humility: "I need God."

CHAPTER 6

The Hungry Pastor

"Blessed are those who hunger and thirst for righteousness, for they will be filled."
—Matthew 5:6

Every few years, my wife and I go on a diet. Neither of us particularly enjoys dieting, but we do it for our health and because the discipline required for a diet usually bleeds over into other areas of our lives. The most frustrating part of a diet is not necessarily what you eat while you're on the diet, but what you can't eat. We develop incredibly intense cravings for all of the unhealthy foods we love to eat but no longer can. Sometimes you don't realize how good certain foods taste until you can't have them anymore. There's nothing quite like a diet to make you long for what you don't have.

Longing. Craving. Hungering. These words should describe our desire for God. The Psalms express this sense of longing well:

> As the deer longs for flowing streams, so
> I long for you, God. I thirst for God, the
> living God. (Ps. 42:1–2a)

> God, you are my God; I eagerly seek you.
> I thirst for you; my body faints for you in
> a land that is dry, desolate, and without
> water. (Ps. 63:1)

How would you describe your walk with God? I'm not talking about your encounters with the things of God in your professional capacity as a pastor. I'm talking about your personal relationship with the Lord. Would you describe it as dry, desolate, and without water? Or would you describe it as hungering and thirsting after God? Do you long for the Lord? Do you crave God's manifest presence in your life?

Jesus says, "Blessed are those who hunger and thirst for righteousness, for they will be filled" (Matt. 5:6). Hungering and thirsting for the righteousness that comes from God could simply be described, in the words of A. W. Tozer, as "following hard after God."[1] It is longing for God himself. It's a desire to see God fill your life with what you don't have without his presence. It's a craving for the kind of life only God can produce in you. God will bless the hungry pastor.

I love to hunt, but not all hunting is created equal. Deer hunting in Texas, for instance, is about as boring an activity as you can ever experience. You sit in a deer stand and quietly wait for an unsuspecting deer to wander close enough for you to take a shot. Growing up in Texas, this was the only kind of hunting I knew. When our family moved to New Mexico a number of years ago, my eyes were opened to a new world of hunting. One of my favorite hunts now is an elk hunt. There's no waiting around, no boredom, no passivity. When you hunt elk, you *hunt* elk. You hike for miles, using an elk call to try to identify the location of a herd of elk, and then the fun begins. In an elk hunt, you don't *sit*; you *stalk*. You track the elk until you get that moment of ecstasy when an elk appears in your crosshairs and you consummate the hunt.

I cannot think of a more apropos description of a spiritual pursuit of God. You can either sit or stalk in your relationship with God. You can be passive or active. You can be self-satisfied with what you already have or hungry for what you don't yet have but desperately need. Hunger and thirst for the righteousness only God can give is actually the hinge point of the Beatitudes and of the entire Sermon on the Mount itself.

Where It All Leads

One of the most startling verses in the Sermon on the Mount is Matthew 5:20. Jesus says, "For I tell you,

unless your righteousness surpasses that of the scribes and
Pharisees, you will never get into the kingdom of heaven."
Jesus then begins to define exactly what it means to have
surpassing righteousness. Six times in the subsequent
verses, Jesus says something along the lines of "you have
heard . . . but I tell you." He addresses the issues of anger,
adultery, promise keeping, truth telling, and the treatment
of an enemy (Matt. 5:21–48). In each case, the righteousness of the kingdom is greater than that of the Pharisees.

Not only that, but Jesus also explains the manner in
which the righteousness of the kingdom is to be expressed.
In Matthew 6, Jesus condemns righteous acts that are
done for show, and in Matthew 7, Jesus condemns self-
righteousness. Both describe what true righteousness is
and how it is expressed. Jesus elevates the expectations for
his followers above and beyond the norm and practice of
the Pharisees.

The question every one of us should be asking when
we read Matthew 5:20 is: "How do I get the true righteousness of the kingdom?" But then again, we already
know the answer. The first beatitude reminds us that we
are spiritually bankrupt.

Here's the kingdom conundrum: to enter the kingdom
you must have a true righteousness that surpasses that of
the religious Pharisees, but it's a righteousness you don't
possess and cannot possess on your own.

This is why Matthew 5:6 is so important. Jesus says
we must hunger and thirst after the righteousness that
we don't have (v. 3) but desperately need (v. 20). At this

point, the point of hungering spiritually for a righteousness we cannot produce on our own but without which we won't enter the kingdom, the second half of this beatitude becomes critical. It's a promise. Jesus says, "If you're hungry for it, you will be filled with it." You *will be* filled. This is a promise. Jesus promises to give us what we need, if we simply long for it.

This is a *passive* promise. The righteousness we need is not something with which we can fill ourselves. It's something the God of righteousness himself will do for us. A hunger for righteousness is not the same as trying to earn or achieve righteousness. The Reformers understood this truth well: the righteousness that comes by faith is a passive righteousness, a righteousness *received* not *earned*. Righteousness is achieved *for* us, not *by* us. Theologians call this the doctrine of *imputation*. This is what Paul means when he says, "Faith was credited to Abraham for righteousness" (Rom. 4:9).

Even though this righteousness must be passively received, it must also be actively pursued. It cannot be earned, but it must be sought. It cannot be achieved by you, but it must be received by you.

Matthew 5:6 is the essence of the gospel: you need righteousness you don't have, but if you want it, you can have it if you will find it in Jesus. He will do for you what you cannot do for yourself. He will provide you with what you can never have on your own. In short: *Jesus will satisfy the deepest longings of your heart.*

Here's how the fourth beatitude works with the verses surrounding it. The first beatitude reminds us that we are spiritually bankrupt; we don't have what it takes. This leads us to the posture of the second and third beatitudes: we must be broken over our sin and humble enough—and here we come to the fourth beatitude —to come to Jesus, hungry for him to fill us with the righteousness we lack.

This is the path to spiritual blessing. It is also the path to ministry blessing. Blessing in ministry only comes when you recognize that you don't have what it takes, grieve over it, then become humble enough to realize that we need God to do for us what we cannot do for ourselves. The beatitude of humility leads to the beatitude of hunger. Once we embrace the first three beatitudes, we are ready to be hungry for Jesus to do what only he can do in our lives. And once we get hungry for Jesus like that, he steps in and takes over, filling our lack, providing for our need, doing for us what we cannot do for ourselves.

You Are What You Crave

This promise confronts us with another startling reality: if Jesus promises to fill us if we are hungry and thirsty for his activity in our lives, then we are as close to the Lord right now as we want to be.

Dieticians used to sell their lose-weight-quick programs by telling us, "You are what you eat." The strategy was effective, even if it wasn't all that accurate. It's perhaps

more accurate to say, "You are what you crave." Our appe-
tites really do define us. Our desires reveal our spiritual
health. Martin Luther said, "Whatever your heart clings
to and confides in, that is really your god."[2] James K. A.
Smith elaborates on this idea:

> So in this picture, the center of gravity
> of the human person is located not in the
> intellect but in the heart. Why? Because
> the heart is the existential chamber of
> our *love*, and it is our loves that orient us
> toward some ultimate end or *telos*. It's not
> just that I "know" some end or "believe"
> in some *telos*. More than that, I *long* for
> some end. I *want* something, and want it
> ultimately. It is my desires that define me.
> In short, you are what you love.[3]

What do you hunger for? What consumes your day-
dreams? Do you long for a larger church, a better salary,
prominence, influence, or some version of the American
dream? Or do you long to look like and live like Jesus?

If we hunger for the righteousness only Jesus can produce in us, we will begin to look more and more righteous.
This is *progressive* sanctification. We are *declared* righteous in justification and progressively *made* righteous in
sanctification. In justification, Jesus changes our longings
to be Godward. In sanctification, our longings begin to
shape our lives toward Christlikeness. As we long for the
righteousness of Jesus, the Holy Spirit chips away at the

unfinished marble of our lives and begins to make us look more like Christ. He *fills* us with what we hunger for. If we are hungry for the world, we will look like the world. If we are hungry for Christ, we will look more like Christ.

Are you spiritually hungry? As a pastor, I want to be hungry to be a Jesus man. I want to look, live, serve, and minister like him. We can be full of the things of this world or full of the character of Christ. As Christ himself teaches later in the Sermon on the Mount, we cannot serve both "God and mammon" (Matt. 6:24 KJV).

An older pastor once told me that when you first arrive as pastor of a church, the problems in the church are not there because of you. But once you have been pastoring that church for five years, you have a different level of responsibility for the problems in the church. What he meant was that over time a church will begin to reflect both the positive and negative characteristics of its pastor. After five years or so, you have to own the problems that are in your church. There's a lot of truth to that. Over time, to some degree, the church I pastor will begin to look like me. What I celebrate, the church will celebrate. What I scorn, the church will scorn. What I love, the church will love. What I long for, the church will long for. If I only care about attendance and budget numbers, that set of values will begin to seep into the congregation. On the other hand, if I long for the Lord and his righteousness in my life, others in the church will begin to long for the same thing. Blessed are the hungry pastors.

If your church members could candidly speak about what they perceive as your greatest values, what would they say? Would any of them say that you hunger for God's righteousness in your life? Would they accuse you of thirsting for God's presence in your ministry? Would they see an example of a man who is following hard after God?

The Grace of Jesus' Righteousness

The reality is that none of us are as righteous as we should be. Although we should hunger for God, we rarely long for him as we should. The beauty of this text is that Jesus' righteousness supplies what we lack. When you don't crave his righteousness, you still *are* the righteousness of God in Christ (2 Cor. 5:21). Jesus has achieved your righteousness for you. We are filled not with our own achieved righteousness, but with the righteousness achieved by Christ.

America's highest zip line is found at the Royal Gorge in Colorado. For our anniversary a few years ago, my wife and I strapped ourselves into a harness and flew a thousand feet from one end of the massive ravine to the other. Nothing stood between us and certain death at the bottom of the gorge 1,250 feet below except for the small harness we clung to with all our might. There was no safety net. If the harness had torn, we would have fallen quickly to our deaths.

For any works-based religion, there is no "safety net" in the case of failure. The best chance anyone has is to try to be as good as they can be and hope it's enough. Not so for believers in Jesus. As true as it is that we are progressively *made* righteous in sanctification, it is first true that we are positionally *declared* righteous in justification. This is the safety net that ensures our security in Christ even when we fail to live up to the righteous standing into which we are called. We are accepted by God on the merit of Jesus' righteousness alone.

Christ has achieved everything necessary for our righteousness. In him, however much we fail to be what we've been declared to be, we are still viewed as righteous by God the Father (Rom. 5:1). In Christ, we are as acceptable to the Father as Jesus is acceptable to the Father. We are robed in his righteousness. When we fail to embody the posture of the Beatitudes, we are still righteous in God's sight. That's the meaning of being "in Christ" (Eph. 1:3–13). As we are hidden in Christ, we are clothed with Christ's righteousness. When God looks at us, therefore, he no longer sees our sin but, rather, Christ's perfect righteousness.

Pastor, rest in this: there is grace in your failure. There is grace when you aren't righteous. There is grace when you aren't what you are supposed to be, either as a disciple or as a pastor. God's grace provides righteousness for the unrighteous who need and desire it. I love the language of Psalm 32:1–2:

> How joyful is the one whose transgression
> is forgiven, whose sin is covered! How joy-
> ful is a person whom the LORD does not
> charge with iniquity and in whose spirit is
> no deceit!

In Christ, our sin is *forgiven, covered, not charged to our account.* Think about it. That time you spoke out of spite from the pulpit—forgiven. That time you spoke behind someone's back—covered. That hospital visit you didn't make but could have—not charged to your account. That time you exaggerated the truth in order to make yourself look better—forgiven. That time you felt jealous at another person's success—covered. That time you failed to give God your best in the study—not charged to your account.

The imputed righteousness of Christ covers you in your failure and fills you when you are empty. This truth frees you to love, obey, and follow God without the constant fear and insecurity of thinking you aren't accepted by him in the case of failure. It frees you to pursue a life of righteousness with joy because you know that you have already been declared righteous.

This recognition also causes us to pursue righteousness with great humility because it is a received rather than an achieved righteousness. In fact, the fourth beatitude's thematic counterpart in the Sermon on the Mount is Matthew 6:1–18.[4] In that section, Jesus cautions his disciples against "paraded" acts of righteousness, specifically the spiritual practices of giving, prayer, and fasting. He warns against "righteousness for show," the kind of righteousness that is put on display "to be applauded by people" (v. 2). We are not to give, pray, or fast so that others will notice how righteous we are. This would be a mockery of the first and fourth beatitudes. We know that any righteousness we possess is an alien righteousness given to us by God himself. Therefore, when we practice acts of righteousness, we do so with humility, so that "your Father who sees in secret will reward you" (vv. 4, 6, 18).

Cultivating Righteousness

The righteousness of Christ in a pastor is both a status given in justification and a calling cultivated in sanctification. Once we receive the gift of Jesus' righteousness, it is our responsibility to allow the Holy Spirit to cultivate the righteousness of Christ in our lives. The Spirit does this as we commit ourselves to the spiritual disciplines. The disciplines required to live the life of faith are as important for pastors as they are for any believer. So, in practical terms, what does it look like to cultivate a life of righteousness as a pastor?

We cultivate righteousness primarily through the spiritual rhythms of *Word* and *prayer.* There are, of course, other spiritual disciplines, such as fasting, giving, silence and solitude, and gathered worship. Yet, when brought to their irreducible minimum, all of the other disciplines are in one way or another an expression of the disciplines of Word and prayer.

Word and prayer are not only central to cultivating personal righteousness, they are the cornerstones of pastoral ministry itself. When the early church appointed the first deacons in Acts 6, they did so to enable the leaders of the church to devote themselves to "prayer and to the ministry of the word" (v. 4). Eugene Peterson frames the entirety of pastoral work under what he calls "a trigonometry of ministry . . . the act of prayer, the reading of Scripture, and the practice of spiritual direction."[5] These are three ways of *paying attention to God*. Peterson defines them this way:

> Prayer is an act in which I bring myself to attention before God; reading Scripture is an act of attending to God in his speech and action across two millennia in Israel and Christ; spiritual direction is an act of giving attention to what God is doing in the person who happens to be before me at any given moment. Always it is God to whom we are paying, or trying to pay, attention.[6]

As important as the act of spiritual direction is, I want to focus on the first two elements of Peterson's "trigonometry of ministry," for none of us can pay attention to what God is doing in the person in front of us at any given moment until we have first attended to God's Word and come to attention before him in prayer ourselves. Word and prayer are the most primary disciplines in the life of the pastor. They are what you give yourself to before any of the other things. Before our public preaching ministry, before pastoral care, before administering the ordinances, before providing leadership and oversight, before counseling, weddings, or funerals, we must come to the ancient path of Word and prayer.

Word and prayer are like spiritual breathing. You breathe the Word in, and you breathe prayer out. There's a rhythm both to our physical and spiritual breathing. We do these regularly, without interruption. Breathe in the Word; breathe out prayer. Over and over again. Just as breathing is necessary for physical life, the Word and prayer are necessary for spiritual life.

Word and prayer are a spiritual *call* and *response*. In jazz music, a beautiful originality and improvisation occur, even a risk taken, as members of a jazz ensemble play a call and response. The trumpet will riff for a moment, improvising on the theme of the music. The saxophonist will then hear the trumpeter's riff and play her own improvisation in response. This call and response are a dance, if you will, around a central theme that binds it all together. God's Word is the call we hear. Prayer is our response to him as we work the theme over in our hearts and minds.

How will you pastor faithfully without the Word and prayer? God's Word gives me instruction about his will for my life and for the church I lead. It also gives me encouragement as I seek to shepherd the flock faithfully. Prayer gives me discernment about his leading and movement in our midst. It gives me the Spirit's power to do what God has called me to do. Prayer allows me to submit my will and ways to God's will and ways.

There are many ways to develop these spiritual rhythms. Personally, I choose to start my day in Word and prayer. I read a predetermined passage of Scripture according to an annual Bible reading plan. I read and reflect on the Word and then respond in a time of prayer. I read a psalm a day as a guide and prompt for my prayers. I usually write my prayers down to help keep me focused and undistracted before the Lord. My wife and I also memorize a couple of Bible verses a week. Memorization drives meditation, as we think upon and converse with the Lord about his Word.

A mentor of mine once told me that I need to approach my personal time with the Lord "selfishly." I didn't understand what he meant at first. He explained that every pastor's temptation is to read the Word with the primary purpose of preparing a sermon for the church. Prayer, if given any time at all, is usually a quick breath of request for God's blessing on the sermon, or worse, relegated only to public times of gathered worship. His explanation stung a little. He encouraged me to come to God's presence through Word and prayer hungry for God to minister to *me* first. Before I can bring a word to the people, I need a word for me. Before I can minister to the people, I need to be ministered to in the presence of the Lord. Before God will put his touch of blessing on my ministry, he must first touch me. It all starts here, with Word and prayer.

Whatever your particular rhythm looks like, start with Word and prayer. Get back to the basics. There is no cultivated righteousness in sanctification apart from these. These are the means the Spirit chooses to use as he fills us with righteousness. Read the Word. Respond in prayer. Get hungry and thirsty. Reap the reward of righteousness.

The Pastor's Time with God

– Michael Catt –

It has been said that the average pastor only spends two or three minutes a day in time alone with the Lord. I don't know how accurate that statement may be, but I do know that spending time alone with God is one of the most gratifying and yet difficult things we do as pastors. The demands on our time are endless. When you consider sermon preparation, funerals, weddings, and other pastoral obligations, it can seem daunting to carve out daily time with the Lord. Add to that the demands of family and other relationships, and we all find ourselves in a time crunch.

Yet we are told to hunger and thirst after righteousness (Matt. 5:6). The psalmist urges us to delight in the Lord, knowing he will give us the desires of our hearts (Ps. 37:4). Years ago, my mentor, Vance Havner, wrote devotionals for his local newspaper. In one of those articles, he wrote about this deeper hunger: "To hunger and thirst after righteousness is a lost experience with most professing Christians—who are too shallow and superficial, or else too fed-up with the lollipops of earth, really to crave deeper blessing. A deep spiritual feast must emanate from a deep hunger and a big appetite!"

What is it that I really hunger after, honestly? Is it for better sermons? Then I need to hunger for God to speak to me through his Word. Is it for the power of the Spirit on my life? Then I need to thirst for righteousness in my daily living. I must admit that there have been times in my ministry when I wanted to grow the church more than I wanted to grow personally. When this happens, we fail to minister out of the overflow. In those times, our ministry is more of a hunger to feed our flesh than to become more like Jesus.

Being like Jesus begins with giving our day to God. When I was a youth pastor, I would encourage students to develop the habit of a daily quiet time by posting a note somewhere they would see it each morning that read: "No Bible, no breakfast." Let's be honest, many of us in the ministry may eat breakfast or have a weekly breakfast with church members, but we've failed to meet God in the morning hours. We start the day without the spiritual nourishment necessary to strengthen our lives.

We must make sure we are pursuing God, not just the thought of him. We can easily begin to place our favorite authors and books on top of our Bibles and read the Bible through the filter of those we agree with. To hunger and thirst after righteousness means that I must put everything under the Word. Scripture must be my filter, my grid for how I think and act. Jesus called his disciples first and foremost to "be with him" (Mark 3:14). It's not about what we do as much as who we are and who we are with that counts. Yes, we have much to do, but in the end being must come before doing. Years ago I heard a statement that I've never gotten over: "God will never use you publicly until he tutors you privately." If we are used without being with him, then it is little more than wood, hay, and stubble.

Mariano Di Gangi captures the essence of the importance of our time with Jesus:

> *Even when we can cite chapter and verse for creation, corruption, predestination, election, vocation, regeneration, justification, adoption, sanctification and glorification, the test of discipleship remains incomplete; we must still deal with the crucial question of our likeness to the Master who is gentle and humble in heart.*[1]

The time you spend being conformed to the image of Christ is never wasted. Remain in him.

CHAPTER 7

The Sympathetic Pastor

"Blessed are the merciful, for they will be shown mercy."

—Matthew 5:7

I 'll never forget meeting Rick and Eloise.[1] It was a Monday morning. They had visited our church the day before. I called Rick to thank him for being our guest and find out if there was any way I could serve them. Ordinarily when I ask this question, people politely thank me for offering but tell me they don't need anything. Rick, however, asked if I could give him and his wife a ride— right then! A little taken aback, I quickly agreed to meet him and give him a ride. It turns out he and his wife didn't have a vehicle and had walked into town to take a shower in a public rest stop. They were on their way back home when I called. I could not have anticipated what happened when I picked them up off the side of the road.

As I drove them home, I began to hear their story. It was a broken story. It turns out Eloise wasn't even married to Rick. They had lived together since she was a young teenager in a little shack behind her parents' house. The place where they lived was barely more than cardboard and construction paper. On our way to their home, I shared the gospel with them. They had never heard about what Jesus had done for them before. As I pulled up in front of the shack they called home, I gave them the opportunity to place their faith in Christ. They were both ready and trusted Christ right there in my car! It was powerful.

I began explaining what they needed to do next. I gave Rick my Bible, encouraged both of them to read it and begin praying, and invited them to get baptized and become a part of our church family. In what is still one of the weirdest experiences of my ministry thus far, as I was talking them through the next steps as new Christians, two police vehicles pulled up to the house and stopped behind my car. They got out of their vehicles and quickly walked toward us with their hands resting on their side-arms. A bit surprised, I rolled down the window and asked if I could help with anything. To make a long story short, they had an arrest warrant for Rick that they were coming to execute. I explained that I was a pastor and told them about the conversion experience that had just happened. They halfway apologetically explained that there was nothing they could do and that I could come see him in jail. The man was set free by Jesus and then arrested by the police within about five minutes!

My first real discipleship meeting with Rick took place behind bars. Eventually, Rick got out of jail, and I baptized him and Eloise. After a few months they moved out of that state. I thought I'd never see them again, until one day, about three years later, Rick walked into my office at the church. I barely recognized him! He was "dressed and in his right mind" (Mark 5:15). The transformation was amazing. He came to thank me for sharing the gospel with him and told me how his life had changed since then. It was unforgettable.

There were many such radical experiences in the gritty, blue-collar New Mexico oil field town where I pastored at the time. In the boom-and-bust atmosphere of the oil patch, those who are willing to rise early and work long days can make a fortune overnight and lose it all just as quickly. I played softball in those days with twenty-somethings who would make six figures and spend it in "riotous living," in the words of our friend King James (Luke 15:13 KJV). They would have a house, a brand-new truck, a speedboat, a motorcycle, and all the other trimmings that come with having too much money and not enough to do with it. With these excesses came deep brokenness. Drug and alcohol abuse were rampant. Many children would wander all day through the neighborhood where our church was located. They were latchkey kids whose parents worked all day only to return home drunk or high in the later hours of the night. The local high school had one of the highest teen pregnancy rates in the country; it even had a nursery for the children of the students. I conducted funerals for more suicides there than I ever have before or since. Prostitution, gambling, and a drug trade were all present in this small, dusty town. There were many incredibly tough moments in the midst of the messiness of people's lives.

These messy ministry moments are daunting. William Willimon reflects on the nature of the ministry task:

> When I think of my congregation and my responsibility for them, I sometimes feel as if I'm standing before the ocean, and then the bishop hands me a teacup and orders, "Start dipping and call me when you are done," lamented one pastor. Sometimes the sheer weight of human need is almost overwhelming.[2]

In the midst of the messiness, what was most needed in those moments was not my self-righteous judgment of their lifestyles but, rather, a ministry of mercy. That's exactly what Jesus calls for in the fifth beatitude: "Blessed are the merciful, for they will be shown mercy" (Matt. 5:7).

If you are called to be a pastor, you are called to a ministry of mercy. God calls us to empathy, compassion, and kindness. He calls us to sympathy toward sinners. There's transformative power in such a ministry.

Identifying as a Sinner with Sinners

It's easy to be judgmental, isn't it? I have often had to catch myself as I've looked down my nose at others who make decisions I wouldn't make, or believe differently than I believe, or live differently than I would live. It can happen before we even realize it. And it doesn't stop there—our opinions about people sometimes bleed into our treatment of them.

Jesus warned against this kind of mentality in Luke 18:9–14 when he told a parable contrasting a proud Pharisee with a humble tax collector. Pharisees were respectable religious leaders. They were the "rule keepers" of the day. In many ways, they were also gatekeepers in society, deciding who was the "in" crowd and who should be marginalized.

There were no more marginalized figures in those days than tax collectors. Tax collectors were despised in the first century. They were in league with Israel's occupiers, the Romans. Tax collectors would never have been featured as the hero in any normal Jewish story. And yet, in Jesus' story, it's the tax collector and not the Pharisee who is seen as being "in the right." Jesus commends the tax collector because in prayer he humbly admits his need for undeserved mercy (vv. 13–14).

In contrast, the Pharisee looks down his judgmental nose at the people around him, lists the reasons God should hear him, and voices a prayer about how much better he is than other people, including the tax collector he was praying beside (vv. 11–12)! The one thing he does not see himself as is a sinner. He serves as a picture of what unmerciful ministry looks like. He's more than tone-deaf. He is deaf to the status of his soul. He fails to see that he is just as sinful as the tax collector!

We will never be ministers of mercy until we see ourselves as sinners in the midst of fellow sinners. The word
for "mercy" used in this beatitude is used only one other
time in the New Testament. Hebrews 2:17–18 says:

> Therefore, he had to be like his brothers
> and sisters in every way, so that he could
> become a merciful and faithful high priest
> in matters pertaining to God, to make
> atonement for the sins of the people. For
> since he himself has suffered when he was
> tempted, he is able to help those who are
> tempted.

This passage is echoed just a couple of chapters later,
in Hebrews 4:15–16:

> For we do not have a high priest who is
> unable to sympathize with our weaknesses,
> but one who has been tempted in every way
> as we are, yet without sin. Therefore, let us
> approach the throne of grace with bold-
> ness, so that we may receive mercy and find
> grace to help us in time of need.

Don't miss this: Jesus is merciful to sinners because
he understands the temptations we experience. Of course,
there is a key difference between Jesus' experience and
ours. Unlike us, he was tempted but never sinned. But
there is something important for pastors to learn here.
Jesus is a high priest who *sympathizes* with sinners because

he understands what we go through. The Greek word for "sympathize" means "to feel what another is feeling." That is the essence of mercy.

If we are going to show mercy to those we serve, we must first realize that we are sinners who struggle with the same things they struggle with. I can identify with the sheep because I *am* a sheep. If I'm going to be a pastor who sympathizes with sinners and shows mercy, I need to see myself as a fellow sinner in the Christian journey alongside the sheep I lead. I can sympathize with those who grieve, because I grieve at times. I can sympathize with those who struggle with temptation because I've had to fight temptation. I can sympathize with those who feel down and depressed because I've felt that way as well.

As pastors, if we cannot admit that we are fellow sinners, that we *are* the tax collector, we will never be able to extend the mercy of Jesus. It isn't easy to be vulnerable with church members about our sin, either in private or in the pulpit. But in order to show mercy, we have to be transparent about the fact that we are not above the sins and struggles of our people.

Jesus made this point in John 8. A group of Pharisees were about to condemn an adulterous woman to death. Jesus stood in front of the woman, and as the embodiment of mercy, protected her. He made a pertinent statement in John 8:7: "The one without sin among you should be the first to throw a stone at her." Everyone who was ready to throw stones at this guilty woman slithered away as they realized their own guilt and the hypocrisy of condemning a woman when they are just as guilty as she was. The story is revealing: the secret to showing mercy to others is first recognizing the need for mercy ourselves.

Extending Mercy to Sinners

Jesus connects the giving of mercy with the receiving of mercy. The promise he makes is that if mercy is given, it will be received (Matt. 5:7). The inverse is also true: those who have received mercy will give mercy. Extending mercy to others is evidence that you've experienced mercy yourself. If you fail to show mercy to another person, it is unlikely that you really understand what it means to experience it yourself.

Later in Matthew's Gospel, Jesus told a parable about a servant who owed ten thousand talents (the equivalent of about 200,000 years' wages) to a king and could not pay his debt. He begged the king for forgiveness. The king had compassion on him and forgave his debt. The servant then went out and found a fellow servant who owed him a hundred denarii (the equivalent of about 100 days' wages) and demanded payment of the debt (Matt. 18:23–35). When the fellow servant begged for forgiveness of the debt, the servant who had been forgiven the much larger debt refused to forgive. Instead, he put the man in prison. Jesus concluded his story by sharing the reaction of the king when he discovered that the man who had been forgiven much refused to forgive little: "You wicked servant! I forgave you all that debt because you begged me. Shouldn't you also have had mercy on your fellow servant, as I had mercy on you?" (vv. 32–33).

This story gives us several insights into the concept of showing mercy. First, notice the connection between the receiving of mercy and the giving of mercy. If you receive mercy, you ought to give mercy to others. It is unreasonable to receive a gift that you then won't share with others who need it as well.

Second, notice the connection of mercy with compassion. The reason the king showed mercy to the servant who owed him was that he felt compassion for the man. As is the case in Hebrews 4:15–16, mercy and sympathy are shown to be twin siblings.

Third, notice the connection between mercy and forgiveness. Showing mercy is refusing to hold them to the consequences they deserve for their failure. That is what it means to forgive. It means releasing someone from receiving the justice their mistakes demand. Showing mercy to another means offering forgiveness for wrongs that have been done. N. T. Wright says:

> Forgiveness is like the air in your lungs. There's only room for you to inhale the next lungful when you've just breathed out the previous one. If you insist on withholding it, refusing to give someone else the kiss of life they may desperately need, you

won't be able to take any more in yourself
and you will suffocate very quickly.[3]

The point is clear: you can't experience forgiveness
without extending forgiveness.

What's fascinating about this particular point is that
in the structure of the Sermon on the Mount, the counterpart for the beatitude about mercy is found in Matthew
5:38–48.[4] In that section of the sermon, Jesus teaches
what forgiveness looks like. In verses 38–41, he stresses
the importance of not exacting revenge, even though the
slogan, "An eye for an eye and a tooth for a tooth" reflected
the normal reaction for those who were hurt. Instead, in
verses 43–48, Jesus tells his disciples to love their enemies
and pray for their persecutors. In the mirrored structure of
the Sermon on the Mount, Jesus is putting on display the
practical expression of mercy. Showing mercy means forgiving those who hurt us, praying for those who persecute
us, and loving our enemies. In the fifth beatitude, Jesus
reminds us that in giving these things to others, we will
receive them ourselves.

Sympathy. Compassion. Forgiveness. Extending to
others what we have received ourselves. These are the
markers of a life of mercy.

Where can we get the resources to show this kind of
mercy? Remember the journey we've made through the
first four beatitudes. We don't have what it takes, but
Jesus does, so we come to him in brokenness and humility,
hungering to be filled with what only he can give. When

we don't feel merciful, Jesus can fill us with the mercy we need to share with others. Harold Senkbeil says that what we share with the flock must come from Christ himself:

> The best we pastors have to give Christ's sheep and lambs doesn't come from within; it comes from him. His love is perfected through us; it reaches its goal when we extend the love we've received from him. We love because he first loved us (1 John 4:11, 19).[5]

There was no more merciful person than Jesus. The Gospels are full of stories of his compassion for sinners. This accusation was common: "This man welcomes sinners and eats with them" (Luke 15:2). In response to these kinds of attacks, Jesus never denied the accusation but, rather, defended his actions by telling stories about lost sheep who were found by their shepherds, lost coins that were discovered by their owners, and prodigal sons who returned to rejoicing fathers (Luke 15:3–32). Once, when Jesus was attacked for eating with Zacchaeus, a tax collector, he responded by reminding everyone around him that "the Son of Man has come to seek and to save the lost" (Luke 19:10).

If we want to become merciful pastors among the messiness of ministry, we need to come to the most merciful man who ever walked the face of the earth. We experience his mercy for ourselves. We ask him for a heart of mercy for others. And then we share with our flock the mercy we have received.

Ministries of Mercy in the Church

In practical terms, what does it look like to show mercy as a pastor? As pastors, we need to think intentionally about developing both merciful ministries and ministries of mercy in our churches. In other words, mercy ought to mark every ministry in our church, and we ought to have specific ministries that exist for the purpose of tangibly extending mercy to others. Let me give a couple of examples of what I would categorize as a "ministry of mercy."

The ministry of pastoral care and counseling is a ministry of mercy. In Ezekiel 34:2–6, the Lord condemns the shepherds of Israel for their lack of care for the flock:

> Son of man, prophesy against the shepherds of Israel. Prophesy, and say to them, "This is what the Lord GOD says to the shepherds: Woe to the shepherds of Israel, who have been feeding themselves! Shouldn't the shepherds feed their flock? You eat the fat, wear the wool, and butcher the fattened animals, but you do not tend the flock. You have not strengthened the weak, healed the sick, bandaged the injured, brought back the strays, or sought the lost. Instead, you have ruled them with

violence and cruelty. They were scattered for lack of a shepherd; they became food for all the wild animals when they were scattered. My flock went astray on all the mountains and every high hill. My flock was scattered over the whole face of the earth, and there was no one searching or seeking for them.

The shepherds were willing to benefit from the flock but were not committed to bless the flock by caring for it. In contrast, consider the example of the supreme Shepherd in Psalm 23. He provides the counterexample of what it looks like to lead, defend, nourish, provide, protect, and care for the sheep:

The LORD is my shepherd; I have what I need. He lets me lie down in green pastures; he leads me beside quiet waters. He renews my life; he leads me along the right paths for his name's sake. Even when I go through the darkest valley, I fear no danger, for you are with me; your rod and your staff—they comfort me.

You prepare a table before me in the presence of my enemies; you anoint my head with oil; my cup overflows. Only goodness and faithful love will pursue me all the days of my life, and I will dwell in the house of the LORD as long as I live.

As pastors, we are called to care for the church. When someone is sick and goes to the hospital, it is a ministry of mercy to visit the hospital and pray with that person. When someone is homebound, it is a ministry of mercy to spend time with those who are isolated and lonely. When someone dies in the church, it is a ministry of mercy to drop whatever else we are doing to go and be with the grieving family and minister to them in the aftermath of their loss. When someone struggles with doubt, discouragement, depression, or defeat, it is a ministry of mercy to meet with them for prayer and encouragement. When a married couple goes through a tough time and is considering divorce, it is a ministry of mercy to share God's Word and wisdom in a pastoral counseling environment. Taking care of the needs of God's flock through pastoral care and counseling is one tangible way to discover the blessing of being merciful.

Another important example of a ministry of mercy would be the compassion ministries of the local church. I mean here the purposeful ministries that are developed for the underprivileged: the homeless, the hungry, the poor, and the needy. Tim Keller says that the church should look to the example of the good Samaritan to mark out its priorities. Like the good Samaritan, "the church of Jesus Christ must squarely face its responsibility for the neighbors lying in the road."[6] There are many ways a church can minister like the good Samaritan in its community.

Every church should have a benevolence fund set up specifically for the purpose of helping those in need. While certain policies should be put in place to make sure no one is taking advantage of the church, the impulse of every pastor and church should be a heart of generosity for the needy. Churches can offer to pay for certain bills or have a stack of gift cards available to help with groceries or gas.

Many churches offer food or clothes pantries to meet the needs of the impoverished in their community. A few years ago, one of our church campuses opened a closet for single moms as well as adoptive families that is always stocked with diapers, baby bottles, and baby clothes.

One of the most blessed experiences I have had throughout my years as a pastor is ministering to the homeless. Whether it is preaching or serving food at a homeless shelter, handing out peanut butter and jelly sandwiches on the streets, or just giving a ride and praying with homeless hitchhikers who need it from time to time, these have been some of the most meaningful interactions I've ever had in my ministry.

Through compassion ministries such as these, and the regular practice of pastoral care and counseling, you can extend the mercy of Jesus to those in your church who so desperately need the sympathy of a pastor who will listen to them and love them like Jesus.

Blessed are the merciful. If we want to embrace the character of Christ, we will always be on the lookout for opportunities to sympathize with and care for sinners. If you are looking for the opportunity, you might be surprised at how often you meet a Rick and an Eloise who are walking along the side of the road in need of a good Samaritan to point them to the hope of Christ.

Compassion Meets the Need

– Bobby Worthington –

The word compassion *is used three times in the Gospel of Luke. The first time it is used is Luke 7:13 when Jesus showed compassion on the widow of Nain by raising her son from the dead and reuniting him with her. The second time it is used is Luke 10:33 in the parable of the good Samaritan when the Samaritan felt compassion for the man who fell among thieves, and he proved to be the neighbor in the story. The third and final time is Luke 15:20 in the parable of the prodigal son when the father felt compassion for his lost son, forgave him, and received him back home. Compassion meets the need in these three uses in the Gospel of Luke. The need of the widow was provision. Jesus not only raised her son from the dead but also reunited him with his mother to meet her need of provision. The need of the man who fell among thieves was physical, and the Samaritan met the physical needs of the man. The need of the prodigal son was forgiveness, and the father met the spiritual need of his lost son, forgave him, and restored him.*

Compassion meets both the physical and spiritual needs of people. I had the privilege of working in the homeless ministry of First Baptist Dallas during the pastorate of Dr. W. A. Criswell. It started when I was a student at Criswell College.

130

I began to minister to homeless men on the streets of Dallas. I realized that they had both physical and spiritual needs. I filled my backpack with sandwiches and gospel tracts. I went to class in the mornings and on the streets in the afternoons. I would give homeless men sandwiches and gospel tracts and ask them: "Has anyone told you that God loves you?" Many of them said no. I would hand them a sandwich and tell them that God sent me to tell them that he loves them. While they ate the sandwich, I would share the gospel with them. Dr. Criswell learned about my street ministry and called me to be the pastor of the homeless ministry at the church in 1983, a ministry I continued leading until 2009.

I learned in ministry to the homeless through the years that compassion meets the need. If we start meeting the physical needs of people, it leads to meeting their spiritual needs. At the two shelters where I ministered through the years, we had food pantries, clothing rooms, and financial assistance for benevolent purposes. There are many stories I could share. I remember ministering to two families that came to the shelter in the early days of my ministry in need of food for their families. They received food for their families but also received the gospel. The matriarchs of these two families received Christ, and it led many in their families to follow their examples. I have had the continued privilege of ministering to these families for many years and officiated the funerals of both matriarchs several years ago.

There are many ways pastors and churches can show compassion and meet the needs of people in their communities. Ministry is done in context. I believe God gives vision to leaders to do ministry in their specific context. People all around us are in need. I am currently the pastor of Lake June Baptist Church in Southeast Dallas. Recently, we provided food for families in our church to help meet the need during the global COVID-19 pandemic. Yearly, we provide Thanksgiving food boxes (including a new blanket and a letter from the pastor) to people in our community in need. Families have come to Christ and to our church through this ministry over the years.

In addition to serving as a pastor, I am a professor at Criswell College. I teach students that compassion meets the need. I tell my students that meeting people's physical needs leads to meeting their spiritual needs. One practical thing I encourage them to do is to tell people why they are meeting the need in their lives. For example, if I purchase a meal for a homeless person, or food for a family, or meet the physical need in another way, I always ask them if I can tell them why I met their need. The reason I do this is to give testimony of the spiritual transformation of the grace of God in my own life. I begin by telling them that the reason I am doing it for them is because of the change that occurred in my life since I received Christ as my Lord and Savior. I tell them that before I received Christ, I was selfish and self-centered, but Christ has changed my life, caused me to love others, and called me to help meet the needs of others. He has caused me to love my neighbor. I tell them that I am doing it because I love him and I love them. This opens the door for dialogue with them about the gospel and leads to gospel conversations with them. Compassion meets the need!

CHAPTER 8

The Pure Pastor

"Blessed are the pure in heart, for they will see God."

—Matthew 5:8

D id you know that a typical chocolate bar contains an average of eight insect parts?[1] Apparently, sometime between when cocoa beans are harvested and when they are developed into the delicious chocolate bars we enjoy, various insects, including cockroaches, find their way into the mix in such a way that they cannot be filtered out. This hard truth makes it difficult to enjoy chocolate. I should have given you a trigger warning before you read this paragraph. Chocolate has been forever ruined for me.

If it's true that a little impurity can ruin an entire batch of chocolate, it is infinitely truer that impurity in the life of a pastor, or any follower of Christ for that matter, will cause ruin. Jesus said, "Blessed are the pure in heart, for

they will see God" (Matt. 5:8). Purity is important in the
life of every believer, but especially so in the life of a pastor. But purity in our lives is impossible on our own. How
can we become pure in heart and receive the blessing of
seeing God?

Pure, In Christ Alone

I remember sitting in my study a few years ago preparing a sermon on Psalm 15. It's a well-known psalm of
David. The first verse asks: "Lord, who can dwell in your
tent? Who can live on your holy mountain?" The rest of
the psalm (vv. 2–5) answers the question:

> The one who lives blamelessly, practices
> righteousness, and acknowledges the truth
> in his heart—who does not slander with
> his tongue, who does not harm his friend
> or discredit his neighbor, who despises the
> one rejected by the Lord but honors those
> who fear the Lord, who keeps his word
> whatever the cost, who does not lend his
> silver at interest or take a bribe against the
> innocent—the one who does these things
> will never be shaken.

The simple answer to David's question is that only the
pure in heart can live in God's presence. Psalm 24:3–4,
which contains a repetition of some of the themes of
Psalm 15, states that point exactly: "Who may ascend the

mountain of the LORD? Who may stand in his holy place? The one who has clean hands and a pure heart."

The gist of my sermon was this: *if you want to be welcomed into God's presence, you'd better pay attention to having clean hands and a pure heart.* As I sat and reflected on my sermon notes, I came to an embarrassing realization—I had prepared a sermon that any good Pharisee could have preached. All law. No gospel. *Be better. Do better. Be pure. Or else!* The problem with what I was asking people to do is that it is impossible.

Only one person ever lived up to Psalms 15 and 24—Jesus. Only one person ever had clean hands and a pure heart—Jesus. Only one person ever merited acceptance into God's presence—Jesus.

We are not accepted into the presence of God on the basis of our own merit, but on Christ's. The New Living Translation makes this clear in its translation of Romans 3:22: "We are made right with God by placing our faith in Jesus Christ. And this is true for everyone who believes, no matter who we are." The hope of our justification is Christ alone.

The only way to be pure in God's sight and, therefore, welcomed into his presence—or in Jesus' terms, the only way to "see God" (Matt. 5:8)—is through faith in Christ. When you receive Christ by faith, you also receive his *imputed righteousness.* The imputation of Christ's righteousness is one of the sweet and precious doctrines of our faith. Romans 4:6 says that the person "to whom God credits righteousness apart from works" is blessed. Second Corinthians 5:21

says, "He made the one who did not know sin to be sin for us, so that in him *we might become the righteousness of God*" (emphasis added). Imputation is when God credits the righteousness of Christ to our account. In his eyes, if we are in Christ, we *are* the righteousness of God.

That doesn't mean our lives are immediately characterized by righteousness. No, the roots of sin go deep into our hearts, and the process of sanctification is progressive. But in Christ we are *positionally* pure in God's eyes. When I run to Jesus for refuge and rescue from my sin, God looks at me and no longer sees me clothed in my sin but, rather, wrapped in the righteousness of Christ.

After we receive the righteousness of Christ *positionally*, Christ then begins to shape his righteousness into us *progressively*. God puts his Holy Spirit inside us, enabling us to become more righteous as Christ lives through us. This process will be perfected in glorification as we are ultimately "conformed to the image of his Son" (Rom. 8:29).

Today we are called to be pure in heart. One day we *will be* pure in heart. But we never can be pure in heart until we first are pure in Christ.

Pure in Motive

Once Christ's purity is imputed to our account, God begins to purify our hearts. He first purifies our *motives*. Without Christ our motives can come from almost anywhere. We can be motivated by the desire to have, the desire to be known, the desire to control, or the desire to earn God's favor through good works. Pastoral ministry isolated from vital connection to Christ can be marked by these motives as well. It doesn't take the typical church member long to discover if a pastor's motives are askew.

Paul commonly defended the purity of his motives. One passage that is fairly representative of what he says elsewhere is 1 Thessalonians 2:3–6:

> For our exhortation didn't come from error
> or impurity or an intent to deceive. Instead,
> just as we have been approved by God to
> be entrusted with the gospel, so we speak,
> not to please people, but rather God, who
> examines our hearts. For we never used
> flattering speech, as you know, or had
> greedy motives—God is our witness—and
> we didn't seek glory from people, either
> from you or from others.

Notice that Paul appeals to the purity of his motives. First, he says that his ministry was not *gushy*: "so we speak, not to please people, but rather God, who examines our hearts. For we never used flattering speech" (vv. 4b–5a). Paul wasn't motivated by people-pleasing. Second, he says that his ministry was not *greedy*: "For we never . . . had greedy motives—God is our witness" (v. 5). Money was not the driving factor for Paul's preaching. Third, he says that his ministry was not *glory-seeking*: "And we didn't seek

glory from people, either from you or from others" (v. 6).
Paul wasn't in ministry for his own glory but for the glory
of Christ. What a model for ministry!

Peter exhorted the pastors of the early church to watch
out for their motives in 1 Peter 5:2–3:

> Shepherd God's flock among you, not
> overseeing out of compulsion but willingly,
> as God would have you; not out of greed
> for money but eagerly; not lording it over
> those entrusted to you, but being examples
> to the flock.

Peter warns pastors to avoid three ministry motives:
*"not overseeing out of compulsion . . . not out of greed for money
. . . not lording it over those entrusted to you."* First, we do not
pastor out of compulsion. Some pastors are momma called
and daddy sent. Peter says we are not compelled to pastor
from any outside influence other than willing submission
to the call of God. Second, we don't pastor for the money.
Anyone who has pastored for five minutes knows there are
easier ways to earn an income. Third, we don't pastor for a
power trip. There's one Lord of the church, and it isn't us!

Why are you in ministry? Why do you do what you
do? Is it the money? Is it power, control, or influence? Is it
pride, ego, or the need for recognition? As pastors, we are
called to be pure in our motives. One driving motivation
ought to characterize us as pastors: "So, whether you eat or
drink, or whatever you do, do everything for the glory of
God" (1 Cor. 10:31).

Pure in Action

God purifies not only our motives but our *actions* as well. David Christie once said that the three great temptations a pastor will face are the temptation to recline, the temptation to shine, and the temptation to whine.[2] These temptations can turn to actions that are impure. Actions of laziness, sloth, pride, arrogance, ingratitude, or complaining can begin to creep into our lives if we aren't careful. Jesus calls us to be pure in heart.

In Matthew 5:27–37, the thematic counterpart to the sixth beatitude, Jesus lists the kind of impurity that is the opposite of being "pure in heart."[3] He mentions the temptation toward lust and adultery (vv. 27–30), the breaking of the marriage covenant through divorce (vv. 31–32), and the closely related sin of breaking an oath (vv. 33–37). All of these actions reflect impurity of heart.

When my son was first learning to play baseball, he had to learn a hard lesson about paying attention. The coach had given him pretty clear instructions about how to be in a "ready position" before the ball was put in play. Before long, a ball came his way when he wasn't paying attention, and the runner advanced extra bases because he missed the ball. The next inning the coach benched him. The lesson was learned. My son didn't enjoy having to watch the game from the sidelines. Ever since that moment, he has done his best to be ready before each and every pitch.

One of the most terrifying possibilities of ministry is that I would disqualify myself through a sinful action and get put on the ministry "bench" or possibly get kicked off the ministry team entirely. Paul warned Timothy to hold on to the faith so that his faith would not be "shipwrecked" (1 Tim. 1:19). Paul spoke from time to time about those who had abandoned him or turned away from the faith (2 Tim. 4:10, 14–16). John spoke of some who "went out from us, but they did not belong to us" (1 John 2:19). Holding a pastoral title or maintaining a pastoral office is no guarantee that any one of us will cross the finish line as a pastor.

If you think it couldn't happen to you, think again. Any one of us is susceptible to any number of disqualifying acts. The doctrine of *total depravity*, which says that we are completely sinful, means that any one of us is capable of anything. "So, whoever thinks he stands must be careful not to fall," Paul tells us (1 Cor. 10:12).

One of the great hurts and disappointments I've experienced in my life and ministry is the number of friends and mentors I've had who have disqualified themselves through sinful, selfish, and stupid choices. Not a single one of these men would have been the kind of pastor I ever would have guessed would do what they did. They wouldn't have guessed it either. In each case, their public falls from ministry were so surprising that I experienced a grief process where an early stage was disbelief. I just could not wrap my mind around the fact that trusted friends and mentors were capable of doing the things they did. But that's where my theology had to be put to work. "All have sinned and fall short of the glory of God" (Rom. 3:23). I'll say it again, you and I are just as capable of doing anything we see others doing. Given certain circumstances, a certain moment, certain conditions, a certain response, any one of us is capable of anything.

This realization ought to be terrifying. It ought to humble us. It ought to cause us to beg God for the purity of heart, motive, and action that only he can produce in us.

Let me give some practical wisdom and advice at this point. The Lord tells us that with every temptation God provides a way of escape (1 Cor. 10:13). There are several ways we can gain victory over temptation and sin.

First, learn to take your thoughts captive (2 Cor. 10:5). Not every bad thought or temptation that enters your mind is sin. Hebrews 4:15 tells us that Jesus was tempted in every way we are and yet he did not sin. This means that not all temptation is sin. Every day, any number of tempting thoughts will cross our minds. When that happens, you have a choice: you can cultivate it to the point of acting on it either in thought or deed, at which point it is sin (James 1:14–15), or you can capture that thought and put it in jail where it can no longer operate in your mind or heart with freedom. The key is to take the thought captive and put it in its proper place before it leads you to sin.

I once heard someone say that tempting thoughts are like stray cats. If you are having coffee on your porch, a stray cat might come rub up against your leg. If you ignore or shoo away the cat, the disturbance will go no further than that. But if you pick up the cat and begin to pet it, it will return the next day and the day after that. When tempting thoughts come to mind, you can pick them up and pet them or you can take them captive and put them on death row.

Second, set up intentional accountability in your life. If you don't have software on your devices to help protect you against the temptation of pornography, stop reading and set something up to provide accountability for your phone and computer. Beyond this, you need to invite a few close and trusted friends or mentors to ask you hard questions on a regular basis. One of my mentors asks me to rate the health of my marriage on a scale of one to ten every time we talk. I know that the question is coming, no matter what other reasons we might have had to talk. When I give my answer, he always presses me to answer why I gave the number I did. These are not always easy conversations, but they do open a door for accountability that I desperately need.

Third, realize that victory over sin is a matter of competing loves. We love our sin, or else we wouldn't do it. We also love Christ. Our *wants* war against each other. Paul expresses this dynamic in Galatians 5:17: "For the flesh desires what is against the Spirit, and the Spirit desires what is against the flesh; these are opposed to each other, so that you don't do what you want." We want to follow Christ, but we also want our sin. We win victory over sin when our love for Jesus is greater than our love for our sin.

Fourth, learn the power of prayer in the moment of temptation. In a moment of temptation, if you will begin immediately praying, you will be amazed at how quickly the mind and heart shift from the tempting thought toward the Lord. Jesus taught us to pray to the Father: "Do not bring us into temptation, but deliver us from the evil one" (Matt. 6:13). Scripture tells us that the Holy Spirit is our "Helper" (John 14:26 esv), and Jesus is our "advocate" (1 John 2:1). That means not one of us faces temptation on our own. We can pray to the Father for deliverance, to the Spirit for help, and to Jesus for intercession. All three persons of our triune God stand ready to come to our aid in temptation. He can make us pure in heart.

The common saying that God will never give us more than we can handle is not true. But it is true that God will never give us more than *he* can handle! Paul says, "No temptation has come upon you except what is common to humanity. But God is faithful; he will not allow you to be tempted beyond what you are able, but with the temptation he will also provide the way out so that you may be able to bear it" (1 Cor. 10:13). When we are tempted to impure motives or actions, we can say with the psalmist: "My help comes from the Lord, the Maker of heaven and earth" (Ps. 121:2).

Personal Purity in a Public Pastorate

– Juan Sanchez –

"My people's greatest need is my personal holiness." This quote, attributed to Scottish pastor Robert Murray M'Cheyne (1813–1843), aptly summarizes the thrust of Paul's exhortations to Timothy. In a context in which false teachers had arisen within the church threatening to lead members astray, Paul urged Timothy to "have nothing to do with irreverent, silly myths. Rather train yourself for godliness" (1 Tim. 4:7 ESV). This pursuit requires toiling and striving (1 Tim. 4:10). And not only is Timothy to "command and teach these things" (1 Tim. 4:11), but he is also to "keep a close watch on [himself] and on the teaching. . . . For by so doing [he] will save both [himself] and [his] hearers" (1 Tim. 4:16 ESV). Our people's greatest need is a personal holiness that flows out of the teaching of the gospel.

Naturally, this raises the question as to why. Why is a pastor to prioritize holiness? In short, because we lead by example. The apostle Peter, an elder himself, urged the elders of the churches in Asia Minor to "shepherd the flock of God that is among you, . . . being examples to the flock" (1 Pet. 5:2–3 ESV). In other words, shepherds are to be "followable." I know that's not a word; I just made it up. But it captures the manner in which we are called to lead—by example. This should come as no surprise to anyone who has read the Bible. The history of Israel makes clear that as its kings and prophets and priests went, so did the nation. Tragically, Israel's leaders led them into judgment and exile. Thankfully, Jesus is the promised King, Prophet, and Priest who came to restore Israel. He is the answer to Israel's exile (Matt. 1:1–17). By retracing Israel's steps out of Egypt (Matt. 2:15) and through the wilderness wandering (Matt. 4:1–11), Jesus led a new exodus and rescued his people out of slavery to sin. Jesus accomplished the promised salvation by fulfilling the covenant Israel broke. He kept the law perfectly, winning the blessings of obedience, and he received the curses of disobedience by hanging on a cross, paying the penalty for transgression (Gal. 3:10–14).

Our job as pastors is to proclaim this Jesus, "warning and teaching everyone with all wisdom so that we may present everyone mature in Christ" (Col. 1:28). How do we do that? Clearly, by teaching the gospel. But also by our example. Our message falls on deaf ears if our lives contradict it. That is true for the watching, unbelieving world, which is why Peter declares: "Beloved, I urge you as sojourners and exiles to abstain from the passions of the flesh, which wage war against your soul. Keep your conduct among the Gentiles honorable, so that when they speak against you as evildoers, they may see your good deeds and glorify God on the day of visitation" (1 Pet. 2:11–12 ESV). We prioritize personal purity for the sake of the gospel and the name of Christ as we live in a skeptical world.

But we also prioritize personal purity, as Paul reminded Timothy, for the sake of our own souls and the souls of those we lead (1 Tim. 4:16). As we go, so will the church. Consequently, we are to be "above reproach," living pure and holy lives. That is, live in such a way that when accusations fly, they won't stick (1 Tim. 3:2). We are to be above reproach in our personal lives, in our family lives, in our spiritual lives, and in our public lives (vv. 1–7). Why? Because our people are listening to our teaching, and they are watching our lives—how we live, how we spend our money, how we treat our wife, how we parent our children. Our people's greatest need is our personal holiness.

CHAPTER 9

The Reconciling Pastor

"Blessed are the peacemakers, for they will be called sons of God."

—Matthew 5:9

Truett Cathy, the founder of Chick-fil-A, tells the story of two men who were rival newspaper publishers in Georgia. They couldn't stand each other. Through somewhat dubious means, Cathy arranged for both men to arrive at his restaurant separately and unaware of the other's presence. Once they got there, they were stunned to see each other.

Before either man had a chance to leave, Cathy convinced them to sit down at a table and try his chicken sandwich, which they agreed to do once they found out that he would purchase a full-page ad in each of their newspapers if they would agree. The ad? A picture of the two men sitting and eating together with the caption: "We disagree on many things, but this is one thing we agree on—this is the best chicken sandwich that we've *ever* eaten."[1]

"Blessed are the peacemakers," Jesus said, "for they will be called sons of God" (Matt. 5:9). Truett Cathy learned that sometimes all it takes to bring people together is courage and a plate of chicken.

The question I want to address in this chapter is: What does it mean to be a peacemaking pastor? I'm going to argue that one of the most important responsibilities of any pastor, or any believer for that matter, is to be committed to the ministry of reconciliation. A peacemaking pastor is a reconciling pastor. He seeks to reconcile people to God and to one another.

The Ministry of Reconciliation

God has given us a ministry of reconciliation. Consider what Paul says in 2 Corinthians 5:18–20:

> Everything is from God, who has reconciled us to himself through Christ and has given us the ministry of reconciliation. That is, in Christ, God was reconciling the world to himself, not counting their trespasses against them, and he has committed the message of reconciliation to us.
>
> Therefore, we are ambassadors for Christ, since God is making his appeal

through us. We plead on Christ's behalf,
"Be reconciled to God."

If you reduce pastoral ministry down to its most essential task, you could say it is peacemaking. The primary task of pastoral ministry is reconciliation. Our ministry should be about vertical and horizontal reconciliation, the reconciliation of people to God and people to one another. Every other pastoral task is for this purpose: to see people come to peace with God and live in peace with one another. The aim of every sermon, every counseling session, every pastoral interaction is at its bottom an attempt to see people united to Christ and Christ's people. God's plan is "to bring everything together in Christ" (Eph. 1:10). As pastors, our aim is to see the lost united to Christ and the saved united to one another.

Peacemaking pastors seek to bring people to peace with God and into peaceful fellowship with God's people. That's what it means to be a reconciling pastor. Pastors stand in a long line of men God has used for this purpose. Indeed, the pastoral office finds its heritage in the Old Testament priesthood.

The Pastor's Priestly Ministry

The pastor finds his archetype not in the Greek orator but in the Hebrew prophet and the Levitical priest. Though there are fascinating parallels between the ministry of pastor and the ministry of prophet, particularly for the task of preaching, the priestly nature of the pastorate is what I'm discussing here.

The priests of the Old Testament had a special calling. They were set apart by ordination for the purpose of serving the Lord and his people. Leviticus 8 describes the ordination of Aaron and his sons. Moses put blood on their right earlobes (signifying their need to *listen* to God), their right thumbs (signifying their *service* to God), and the big toes on their right feet (signifying their call to *walk* with God). This ordination set them apart to serve as a man of God, not unlike the pastoral "laying on of hands" in the New Testament (Acts 13:3; 1 Tim. 4:14).

The Levitical priests also had a sacred responsibility. They were called to stand before God on behalf of the people and stand before people on behalf of God. Their task is defined in Deuteronomy 10:8:

> "At that time the LORD set apart the tribe of Levi to carry the ark of the LORD's covenant, to stand before the LORD to serve him, and to pronounce blessings in his name, as it is today."

Priests were concerned with the reconciliation of people to God. They were tasked with the responsibility of offering daily, seasonal, and annual sacrifices so that God's wrath would be propitiated and the people could live at peace with him. They would "stand before the Lord" by offering these substitutionary sacrifices on behalf of the people. They represented people to God. They would also represent God to the people and "pronounce blessings in his name." Pastors, likewise, represent the people to God and God to the people. The pastor's business, according to Jonathan Edwards, "is either to act in the name of God's people towards God, or in the name of God towards the people."[2]

Priests were also concerned with the reconciliation of people to one another. An Israelite could be removed from the community for any number of reasons. For instance, if someone became leprous, they would be put outside the camp of the Israelites. There they would live on the margins of society, separated from the community of God's people. The pathway to reentry into the life of the community went through the priest. The priest would perform a ceremonial purification ritual so that a leper could be restored and reconciled to the community (Lev. 14:1–32).

The priestly task of the Levites was, at a foundational level, peacemaking. Unlike a prophet who could deliver a message and depart as soon as it was delivered, the priests lived close to the people and conducted a ministry of touch. Their hands would have been stained with the blood of animal sacrifices as they sought the people's reconciliation to God. Their hearts would have been saturated with compassion as they reconciled marginalized people back into the people of God.

This dual responsibility—of being a conduit for vertical *and* horizontal reconciliation—serves as the model for pastoral peacemaking. Pastors stand in the tradition of the priesthood as ministers of the new covenant. We are ministers of the gospel of reconciliation so people can be reconciled to God and restored to the community of God's people. We are a "Kingdom of priests" (Rev. 1:6 NLT). The New Testament vision for the church is that of a reconciling community. The pastor is called to be the lead reconciler in the church, concerned with people's peace with God and with one another.

This provides a dual mandate for pastoral ministry: in the midst of other priorities, we are to lead well in *evangelism* and in *conflict resolution*. A biblically faithful pastor is an evangelistic pastor. If we care about peacemaking between God and people, we will "do the work of an evangelist" (2 Tim. 4:5). We will do everything we can to see people who are far from God come to have "peace with God" (Rom. 5:1).

We also will be committed to making peace among people. Church hurts are real. It's not a question of if, but when people are going to hurt one another deeply in our churches. Sometimes church hurts are over big issues that really matter. Just as frequently, they are over small issues that become big issues because they are not addressed. They fester until a molehill becomes a mountain. Pastors who are unskilled in conflict resolution and interpersonal reconciliation won't last long in ministry. The pastor has the priestly ministry of working to reconcile people to one another in the aftermath of church hurts and fights. Pastors must be willing and able to do the hard work and the heart work of resolving conflicts and winning peace in the church.

Winning the Peace

Winston Churchill was one of the greatest wartime leaders in history. Long before anyone else saw the existential threat Nazi Germany posed to Western civilization, Churchill had been sounding warning bells about the threat of Hitler's growing power. When Hitler began his sweeping advance across Europe and came to the precipice of invading Great Britain, Churchill stood alone against him. If not for Churchill's courage in the face of what seemed then as near certain defeat, history would have taken a dark turn. The war could not have been won without Churchill's astonishing leadership.

It is stunning, then, that on July 26, 1945, Churchill lost his bid for reelection as the British prime minister. The man who had alone stood against tyranny to save not only his own nation but the entire world from Nazi Germany was rejected by his own people. One of the reasons for his loss, as noted at the time, was his decision to engage in bitter party politics. At one point, Churchill referred to the Gestapo in reference to the policies of his political opponents. After his embarrassing loss, the *Times* of London said: "Mr. Churchill himself introduced and insisted upon emphasizing the narrower animosities of the party fight."[3] Divisive partisanship, it seems, was Churchill's downfall. The man who won the war could not keep the peace.

On the landscape of recent Baptist history, two conflicts loom large. Though separated by an ocean and a period of one hundred years, there are many similarities between the Downgrade Controversy in which Charles Spurgeon was engaged with the Baptist Union in Great Britain and the Battle for the Bible in the Southern Baptist Convention in the last quarter of the twentieth century. In both cases denominational liberalism was on the rise. In both cases a group of conservative pastors sought to recover biblical fidelity within the denomination. Spurgeon's case failed and was forced to leave the Baptist Union. In the case of the Southern Baptist Convention, the conservatives succeeded but, in the process, lost both liberal and conservative pastors and churches that did not want to be part of a denominational fight.

Some pastors are proficient at winning theological or ecclesiological battles. Pastors are not always prepared to win the peace. There are times pastors need to be willing to fight a theological battle. There are also times when pastors must be able to preserve the peace. It takes wisdom to know the difference.

There are times when a fight is inevitable and unavoidable. Sometimes the fight seeks you rather than the other way around. I have experienced the shock of a staff-led church split. That kind of conflict is something for which you can never be prepared. It blindsides you. It bruises your soul. The scars last long after the fight is over.

A pastor of character is never eager for a fight. Ready to stand for truth? Absolutely. Ready to take a punch, if need be, for the gospel? Yes! Eager for conflict? God forbid.

Are you as ready to fight the battle for peace as you are to fight other battles? One of the qualifications for a pastor is that he not be "quarrelsome" (1 Tim. 3:3). We must be marked not merely by the courage to do battle when necessary but also the gentleness, wisdom, and endurance needed to win the peace. Jesus said the peacemakers are blessed (Matt. 5:9).

As a pastor, I want to embrace the eschatological vision of Isaiah 2:4:

> He will settle disputes among the nations
> and provide arbitration for many peoples.
> They will beat their swords into plows and
> their spears into pruning knives. Nation
> will not take up the sword against nation,
> and they will never again train for war.

One day Jesus will return to make all things new. At that time weapons of war will be reshaped into gardening tools. There won't be a need for weapons anymore because every conflict will end. This is an eschatological reality to which we all look forward. But it is an already/not-yet reality that can take shape within the people of God now. We ought to be able to say with the psalmist, "I am for peace" (Ps. 120:7).

What happens when you are a peacemaking, reconciling pastor? Jesus says the peacemakers will be called "sons of God" (Matt. 5:9). If we become peacemakers, we will bear the name the ultimate Peacemaker bears—"Son of God." Jesus is the "Prince of Peace" (Isa. 9:6). We are called "sons of God" when we make peace because making peace is what the Son of God came to do. We will be called what he is called because we will be doing what he came to do.

The Posture It Takes

So, what does it take to make peace within the church? How can we be agents of reconciliation as pastors? I'd like to share several principles for peacemaking with you.

First, as every young parent quickly learns to do with their children, you have to pick your battles carefully. A pastor should be reluctant to fight. Paul says a pastor must not be "a bully but gentle, not quarrelsome" (1 Tim. 3:3). Not everything is worth a fight. Not every issue is a hill on which to die. There are "issues," and then there are "splitting issues." Not everything is a splitting issue. Joel Gregory once told the story of an Irishman who was entrusted by his lord with the task of guarding a castle. He decided to build a wall around the castle to protect it. His lord returned to find a big wall but the castle had disappeared! The Irishman had used the stone from the castle to build the wall. The point is clear: if we pick the wrong battles, we may destroy the castle while building the wall.[4] Sometimes church members fight battles to protect the church, but end up dividing and destroying the church in the process.

Which battles are worth fighting? Albert Mohler suggests using a system of "theological triage" to parse out theological issues into primary, secondary, and tertiary categories.[5] Primary theological issues are those issues of theological orthodoxy which determine who embraces Christian faith and who does not, such as the divinity of Christ and the necessity of faith in Jesus for salvation. Secondary issues are "in the family" doctrines where fellow Christians can disagree about matters that do not separate believer from unbeliever but are serious enough to divide Christians into different denominational groups. For the sake of the unity of the broader church, it may be more unifying in the long run to worship in separate churches so that you are not constantly fighting about baptism or church government. Primary and secondary issues can be considered "splitting" issues. Tertiary issues are those matters of lesser importance about which Christians can disagree and remain in the same church together, agreeing to friendly disagreement and dialogue about such matters as end-times views or views of God's sovereignty and man's free will.

Not everything is worth a fight. Ken Sande says:

> There are many conflicts that require a lot of time and effort to resolve. But there are far more that can be resolved simply by overlooking minor offenses or relinquishing rights for the sake of God's kingdom. Therefore, before focusing on your rights,

take a careful look at your responsibilities.
Before you go to remove the speck from
your brother's eye, ask yourself, "Is this
really worth fighting over?"[6]

Much conflict can be avoided in the church by simply
choosing not to make a mountain of every molehill.

Second, embrace a Christlike spirit toward those with
whom you disagree. Unfortunately, within the church we
sometimes treat "debate as war" and those with whom
we disagree as enemies rather than neighbors.[7] One of
the solutions, according to Baylor University professor
Alan Jacobs, is to learn how "to cultivate a more general
disposition of skepticism about our own motives and generosity toward the motives of others."[8] In some church
fights, we tend to do exactly the opposite. Worse than
that, few people are willing to have a good-natured disagreement and remain friends once it's over. They aren't
satisfied until their ideological opponent is destroyed.
Victory at all costs is the mantra. Diminishing another
human, an image-bearer of God, and losing your own
humanity in the process is a high price to pay to win an
argument. Jacobs suggests that by adopting a more generous disposition toward one another, many fights might
be avoided altogether. A healthy community, he notes, is
marked by "people who are not so much like-minded as
like-hearted."[9] If we could learn to value like-heartedness
as much as like-mindedness, we would have much more
peace in the church.

In a recent history of Gateway Seminary, authors Chris Chun and John Shouse include an anecdote from Barry Stricker, a former faculty member, about a debate that once took place between Bill Hendricks and Dale Moody about the doctrine of the perseverance of the saints:

> For several hours, Dr. Hendricks and Dr. Moody, with humor and passion, demonstrated to our student body how believers can disagree about crucial matters and still remain friends. Following their heated debate, Dr. Moody and Dr. Hendricks went and enjoyed lunch together. That's the sort of thing that happened often in those days, and the students were richer for it.[10]

Third, if you are going to be a pastor marked by the spirit of reconciliation, it's going to take a deep level of commitment. Peacemaking is hard. I shared this story earlier, but it is worth repeating. Once, when I was experiencing a season of conflict in a church, I asked a wise, older pastor for advice. He shared something I'll never forget. He said, "Andrew, if you face an opponent, agitator, or antagonist in a church conflict, you ought rarely to draw your sword. But if you draw it, make sure you are the last one standing. Then, have enough love and dedication for the church to stay for a decade afterward to put the pieces back together." That's intense. It takes a certain robust fortitude to survive a church fight and then stick it out long enough to make peace afterward.

Fourth, learn to be "quick to listen, slow to speak, and slow to anger" (James 1:19). This is exactly what Jesus says in the Sermon on the Mount. He doesn't leave us in the dark about the kind of posture we need to take if we are going to be peacemakers. In short, an attitude of anger is one we absolutely must reject if we are going to be agents of reconciliation. In the seventh beatitude's counterpart in the Sermon on the Mount in Matthew 5:21–26, Jesus speaks to the importance of casting aside angry attitudes and embracing reconciliation.[11] Jesus clarifies the meaning of the Old Testament law. "Do not murder" is part of the Mosaic law. Jesus interprets this to mean not only not to kill someone but not even to be angry or insulting to another person (v. 22). Beyond this, Jesus urges his disciples to seek reconciliation with a brother or sister with whom they might be at odds. He prioritizes the pursuit of reconciled relationships above even the offering of a gift at the altar in worship (vv. 23–24).

Fifth, become an expert in forgiveness. Charles Williams, one of the members of the famed Inklings of Oxford, once described Jesus as "forgiveness in flesh."[12] As a believer and as a pastor, you are never more like Jesus than when you give and when you forgive. Pastoral ministry provides us with many opportunities to forgive. When we do, the Lord uses it in our lives to shape us into Christlikeness. Blessed are the peacemakers.

Peacemaking is beautiful. In my first full-time pastorate, I served in a rural part of Texas where there were more cows than people. Amy and I formed such wonderful relationships shepherding this small congregation of farmers and ranchers. After about a year as pastor, I encountered a conflict. A woman in the church became upset with me when I failed to make it to a birthday party to which she had invited me. Even though we had a good relationship prior to that missed opportunity, my failure to come to the party made her upset with me. She started looking for a chance to criticize me.

It wasn't long before an opportunity came. This woman called the chairman of deacons to tell him that I had not visited another woman in our church who happened to be in the hospital at the time. The deacon chairman then called me to share the complaint. The only problem was that I *had* made the hospital visit. She had shared something false about me.

I immediately called the woman whose party I had missed and began the process of getting to the bottom of what was happening. As is usually the case, the initial issue that seemed to be causing the conflict was not the real issue. It didn't take long before I found out that this woman had been hurt that I had missed her party. She admitted that she was frustrated with me and wanted to try to get back at me in some way. She apologized on the phone, and I apologized for missing the party. We agreed to forgive each other and move past this little speed bump in the road of our relationship.

The next day this woman knocked on the door of the country parsonage where we lived. I opened the door, and there she was with a smile on her face and a loaf of home-made bread in her hands. She explained that it was Amish friendship bread, and she baked it for me as a symbol of our deeper friendship as a result of having made it through a conflict in a peaceful way. Pastor, I'll tell you this: peace-making is a hard and arduous task in ministry, but once you've made peace, it tastes wonderful.

How to Bring Healing to a Hurting Congregation

– Clint Pressley –

It's been my experience that churches are like people in that they have personalities, emotions, and a past. They suffer loss, feel abused, deal with anxiety, and oftentimes, a sort of collective depression. Whether it's decline, division, or just hurt, many churches across our country need revitalization, or better said, they need pastors that will shepherd with enthusiasm. I'd like to offer ten suggestions on leading a church out of decline, division, or just plain hurt.

First, embrace joyful exposition. At the beginning of your ministry with a damaged congregation, let them know you are going to preach through books of the Bible and then do so with great, intangible joy. You may start with Philippians or 1 John or Genesis. Let the congregation experience your passion for God's Word, your trust in its sufficiency, and your utter joy in studying it. That passion will be contagious and will be driven not by personality but by the Bible's authority.

Second, become an expert on the church. It's been my experience that a church's history can give a good anchor, in part, to the current situation. I once pastored a deeply divided and damaged congregation, and one of the first things I did was to read every newsletter, Sunday school bulletin, and business meeting minutes I could find. That exercise gave me a better feel for "how we got here." Not only that, but our people knew I was doing that, and they seemed to appreciate my interest.

Third, clean the place up. Many times the appearance of the church will reflect a downward trajectory. Sometimes this can be easily remedied with an edger and power washer. A neglected building could be symptomatic of a suffering congregation, and caring for the physical plant sends a message about the future.

Fourth, work within the system. Every congregation has its own way of doing things—constitutions, bylaws, committee structures, and approach to business meetings. For the first several years, I would work within the system, even if it was clunky and archaic. The system changes will come in time. At first, deal with the ministry of souls.

Fifth, genuinely love the people. There is absolutely no substitute for your actively loving the people you serve, individually and collectively. Ask God to fill you with love and then find ways to express that love. "Love covers a multitude of sins" (1 Pet. 4:8), and in the church context, the more they know you love them, the further they will follow you down the road.

Sixth, celebrate the respectable traditions; tolerate the others. Many churches have strong traditions that serve a great purpose. I served a church once where there was the tradition that after the funeral service the men of the church would cover the grave by hand, each with his own shovel. It built a strong bond and was a good reminder of our own mortality. I celebrated that tradition. There are plenty of other traditions in a church, however, that are downright weird. For a time, I *would tolerate those traditions, asking God to use his Word and time to take care of those.*

Seventh, be consistent. A damaged church is slow to trust a new pastor. Genuine consistency in the pulpit, home life, and pastoral ministry will go a long way in building trust. Trust takes time and proof that you mean what you say. Show up on time, return phone calls, make the visits, work hard in the study, and preach with intensity. Over time, trust will translate into a willingness to follow.

Eighth, live in hope. A damaged and hurting church is a "hope black hole" and needs a pastor to reignite their hope in the power of the gospel and the joy of grace. Hope is based on the future but has an effect in the present, and just a little hope, even in a few members, can start the process of breathing life into the church.

Ninth, give yourself to that church. Live as close as you can to the church or in the community, be as accessible as you can tolerate, and spend your time personally investing in your people. A pastoral connection to a hurting church infuses them with a sense of value and direction. It also sends the signal that you genuinely desire to be one of them, even if that never actually comes to pass.

Tenth, thank God for your church and pray for its health. The church you serve is a privilege, a local body of believers, God's adopted children. And you need to give thanks to God for your church. We are grateful for what we value, and the church has been infused with value by the blood of Jesus. As you thank God for your church, intercede, asking God to do specific and drastic things in that congregation, knowing that to serve the church as pastor is the pinnacle of privilege.

The above suggestions are just that, suggestions, but they are from experience. I pray they will be of some help as you seek to lead a church toward healing.

CHAPTER 10

The Enduring Pastor

*"Blessed are those who are persecuted because
of righteousness, for the kingdom of heaven is
theirs. You are blessed when they insult you and
persecute you and falsely say every kind of evil
against you because of me. Be glad and rejoice,
because your reward is great in heaven. For that
is how they persecuted the prophets who were
before you."*

—Matthew 5:10–12

As I write this, churches across the world are in the
throes of a global pandemic. COVID-19, a disease
that was unknown just a few months ago, has disrupted
churches, businesses, and national economies around the
world. Nearly every church in America closed their doors
for in-person gatherings and provided online worship

services for nearly three months. To say these are uncharted waters would be the understatement of a generation.

In the midst of this pandemic, a viral video of the brutal death of an African American man named George Floyd by a white police officer spread around the globe. This set off hundreds of protests in cities across America and even in other countries. Many of these protests were peaceful, but others turned into violent riots where several people lost their lives and many people experienced the destruction of their property.

It's difficult to put into words the stress, sorrow, struggle, and division that have marked this period in our country's history. The level of sheer animosity, partisanship, and vitriol that has characterized our nation is stunning. Social media has only added fuel to the fire.

Tensions have not been this high in a long time, both in the country and in churches. People are divided politically, racially, socioeconomically, and even spiritually.

Pastors Have Feelings, Too

Pastoral ministry during this time has been a challenge. Pastors have been in the crucible of trying to navigate problems for which no seminary class could have ever prepared them. Personally, this has been the hardest period of ministry in my life.

Not only is there the leadership challenge of trying to figure out how to lead a church when you cannot gather in person, or make hospital visits, or even be within six feet of others (due to social distancing, a term few people had ever heard before the pandemic), but there is the challenge of leading a church filled with people whose opinions about pandemics, politics, and protests span the spectrum.

The criticism pastors have experienced during this season has been overwhelming. When the pandemic first came to my local community, for instance, I began to receive emails, letters, and text messages telling me that if our church continued gathering in person for worship I would be responsible for deaths in our city because the virus would spread in our meeting, and if we decided to gather, it was a sign that I did not care about people.

Then, when we decided not to gather in person due to restrictions put on us by our local government, I began to receive messages from people who thought I was operating on fear rather than faith, and if I trusted God enough, we would continue to meet in person. One person wrote me a letter calling me "a lackey of Satan" for shifting to online ministry and not providing in-person worship opportunities for a season.

I received some of the vilest letters and messages I have ever received in fifteen years of ministry. I routinely heard from people who told me that my decisions were disappointing, that I had failed them as a pastor or had let them down by either being too cautious or not being cautious enough. Each criticism was put in the starkest terms. *You're going to cause deaths in our city because you are meeting. You don't really have faith in God because you aren't meeting.* And

all of this from those *within* the church. Many more outside the church leveled all kinds of accusations and blame
on pastors and churches during this time.

There have been many days when the temptation to
quit has been strong. I've thought about wearing a shirt
that says: "Pastors have feelings, too!" I know of many
pastors who feel the same way. The crucible of criticism is
difficult. Sometimes you can't win for losing. There is no
precedent for how to lead a church through a global pandemic, and yet everyone seems to know the right way to
lead (except for the pastor, of course). Many church members seem to have forgotten the humanity of their pastors.

Ministry Is Tough

Of course, this is not the first time I've experienced
criticism or opposition. These things are part and parcel
with ministry. It should not be surprising to us that there
are antagonists in the church. Kenneth Haugk defines
"antagonists" as:

> individuals who, on the basis of nonsub-
> stantive evidence, go out of their way to
> make insatiable demands, usually attack-
> ing the person or performance of others.
> These attacks are selfish in nature, tearing
> down rather than building up, and are fre-
> quently directed against those in a leader-
> ship capacity.[1]

Ministry is tough. John McCallum says, "God calls some pastors into churches that feel more like enemy territory than safe-haven."[2] Church hurts are real, and church life is tough for a pastor. Mike Tyson once famously said, "Everybody has a plan until they get punched in the mouth." Many pastors have no idea how many punches they are going to take in ministry.

If you have experienced hurt and pain in your pastoral ministry, I sympathize with you! Here's good news: so does Jesus! He knows what it's like to be hurt by those you serve. He was "despised and rejected by men, a man of suffering" (Isa. 53:3). Not only does Jesus sympathize with shepherds who suffer and sorrow, but he prepares us for it.

The eighth and final beatitude of the Sermon on the Mount in Matthew 5:10–12 confronts us with a hard, uncomfortable truth:

> "Blessed are those who are persecuted because of righteousness, for the kingdom of heaven is theirs.
>
> "You are blessed when they insult you and persecute you and falsely say every kind of evil against you because of me. Be glad and rejoice, because your reward is great in heaven. For that is how they persecuted the prophets who were before you."

If you live for Jesus, your life will become harder, not easier, because of your faith in Jesus. Pastors can bet on it.

Persecution is a normative part of the Christian life. It's a normative part of pastoral ministry.

Now pause and notice that Jesus doesn't give a blanket blessing on those who are persecuted for any reason whatsoever. He says you are blessed when you are persecuted *because of righteousness*. Kent Hughes notes:

> Sadly, Christians are very often persecuted not for their Christianity, but for lack of it. Sometimes they are rejected simply because they have unpleasing personalities. They are rude, insensitive, thoughtless, or piously obnoxious. Some are rejected because they are discerned as proud and judgmental. Others are disliked because they are lazy and irresponsible. Incompetence mixed with piety is sure to bring rejection.[3]

Peter said, "Let none of you suffer as a murderer, a thief, an evildoer, or a meddler" (1 Pet. 4:15). There are no spiritual benefits for enduring hardship because you were a knucklehead. Spiritual blessing comes to those who suffer for the right reasons. Blessed are those who are persecuted because of righteousness.

For some of you who are reading this, this particular beatitude is a tough pill to swallow. It may even sound contradictory. Suffer for righteousness? In the Western church, we have trouble associating suffering with the righteous life. We assume, per the so-called "prosperity gospel," that if we live a righteous life, God will reward us with prosperity and ease. You might negotiate with God: "God, look at all I've done to serve you. Can't you reward my sacrifice with pain-free living?"

Scripture never promises life without pain. Quite the opposite. Paul says, "All who want to live a godly life in Christ Jesus will be persecuted" (2 Tim. 3:12). Peter's first epistle refers time and time again to the fact that the church was persecuted not for doing what is wrong, but for doing what is right (see 1 Pet. 2:20; 3:14; 4:14, 16). It's possible to do everything right, both personally and in your ministry, and still be mistreated. You can be a righteous pastor, and your church still might fire you for the wrong reasons. Doing the right things doesn't always mean you won't run into trouble. If you live a righteous life, you will rub some people the wrong way. They may lash out at you because your life is a living witness to the power of a kingdom that subverts their allegiances and desires. The righteous are often persecuted.

What's more, God often uses pain and suffering in our lives as a means of forming us into the image of Christ. God allows us to suffer hurts and loss in life and ministry, but he only takes away from us what would be a loss to keep or a gain to lose. He works *all* things together for the good of those who love him (Rom. 8:28).

Of course, that doesn't make persecution in life or ministry any easier. It hurts when we experience suffering, opposition, or rejection. Jesus describes persecution in three ways in Matthew 5:11: "You are blessed when they *insult* you and *persecute* you and *falsely say every kind of evil against you* because of me" (emphasis added).

First, Jesus says you may be *insulted*. In the Greek New Testament, this word has the sense of being reviled or even shamed. Jesus refers to one such insult in Matthew 5:22, the insult of being called a "fool." Yes, you may get called a name or two in the course of your ministry.

Second, Jesus says you may be *persecuted*. The sense of this word is that some will harass or chase after you in a hostile way. Some people make it their life mission to make your life difficult. Like a dog that chases after you and nips at your heels, they will constantly nip and bite at you.

Third, Jesus says you may have *evil falsely spoken about you*. This means that sometimes people will lie about you. They will spread falsehoods about you. This may be directed toward your character, your motives, or your actions. It may be that people misinterpret something you said or did, or worse, they may misrepresent you intentionally.

Ministry is tough. Yet Jesus says there's a blessing when you suffer for him. Peter says the same thing in 1 Peter 4:14: "If you are ridiculed for the name of Christ, you are blessed, because the Spirit of glory and of God rests on you."

As we think about this beatitude in light of pastoral ministry, I believe the quality it calls for is *endurance*. As pastors we need to be clear-eyed about the fact that pastoral ministry is going to mean persecution and opposition. If we are going to cross the finish line of ministry, we need to be willing to endure whatever hardship comes our way in the course of our pastoral calling. If we are going to embody the character of Christ in pastoral ministry, we need, I argue, tough hides and tender hearts.

Tough Hide, Tender Heart

There are so many junctures in pastoral ministry where it is tempting to quit. We all have a Critical Chris, Divisive Daniel, Negative Nancy, or Frustrating Frank in the churches we serve. As I tell our pastoral interns, ministry would be easy if it weren't for all the people! Truly, pastoral ministry can wear you down. But part of our pastoral call is to "share in suffering as a good soldier of Christ Jesus" (2 Tim. 2:3). We are called to be pastors who endure through hardship. As Winston Churchill said in his shortest, if not most memorable, speech: "Never, never, never give up."

If you are going to last in ministry, you need a tough hide and a tender heart. You need to have the hide of a rhinoceros and the heart of a golden retriever. You need to be tough enough to take a punch and get back up but not so tough that you become cynical. That's a difficult balance to maintain.

Paul exhibited the quality of endurance in his ministry, all while maintaining a heart that was soft toward people. His ministry was a dizzying series of ups and downs, highs and lows. For instance, when Paul and Barnabas traveled to Lystra, they were worshipped as gods one moment and nearly stoned to death the next (Acts 14:8–19). You would think after getting stoned and left for dead that Paul would at least take a sabbatical! Instead, he picks himself up, dusts himself off, and walks to the next town to preach the gospel (Acts 14:20). Paul's normal pattern was to go to a town, preach the gospel in the synagogue until he got kicked out, then go to the market and preach the gospel until he was driven out, then rinse and repeat in the next town. He summarized his experiences in 2 Corinthians 11:24–28:

> Five times I received the forty lashes minus one from the Jews. Three times I was beaten with rods. Once I received a stoning. Three times I was shipwrecked. I have spent a night and a day in the open sea. On frequent journeys, I faced dangers from rivers, dangers from robbers, dangers from my own people, dangers from Gentiles, dangers in the city, dangers in the wilderness, dangers at sea, and dangers among false brothers; toil and hardship, many sleepless nights, hunger and thirst, often without food, cold, and without clothing. Not to mention other things, there is the daily pressure on me: my concern for all the churches.

Paul had what I like to call *gospel grit*. We need a dose of that in our day. Ministry isn't for the faint of heart. The church needs enduring pastors.

I had a recent conversation with one of my pastoral interns about how to exhibit grit when criticized. I shared with him ten lessons I've learned by experience through the years about how to handle criticism in ministry:

1. If we are going to survive in ministry, we have to develop a tough hide while keeping a tender heart. Cynicism can emerge when we are criticized, and cynicism kills.

2. Don't take all criticism personally. Criticism is often more about the one doing the criticism than the one being criticized.

3. Try to discern the critic's motives. There may be a hidden hurt in play. Or, even if done in the wrong way, they may have a good desire at heart (for you or the church).

4. Look for the grain of truth in the criticism. There is always something to learn from criticism. Ask God to show you what is true in what has been said. Have the humility to learn.

5. Disregard what is not true. Hear criticism like you eat fish: eat the meat, spit out the bones.

6. Stay humble. God has something to teach you in every hard moment. How you handle criticism (and conflict in general) is a test of character. It can lead to sanctifying moments in your life and theirs. It also can solidify your credibility as a godly leader if you handle it well without overreacting.

7. Thank the critic for trusting you with their criticism. If someone comes to you with a complaint, it is because they believe you can do something about it. Get worried when they stop coming to you—that means they don't believe you can fix the problem. Thank every critic. Their response will surprise you.

8. Ask God to grow you and make you a wiser leader because of what you've learned through the criticism. Sometimes our critics are right and we are wrong. Ask God to show you this and then teach you how to do better in the future. You will be a better leader as a result.

9. Forgive. Freely you've been forgiven. Freely forgive. If we want a critic's

forgiveness when we err, we need to forgive the critic when they say the wrong thing in the wrong way and hurt us. Give them the benefit of the doubt that this may not be their best moment and show grace.

10. Move forward. Don't live in the past and wallow in the hurt of yesterday. Take the criticism, learn what you can, forget what's hurtful, and focus on what's next. You can't drive forward while always looking in the rearview mirror.

The founding pastor of the church I now serve as pastor was a man named Chester O'Brien. Chester was one of God's sweet saints. I had the privilege of getting to know him before he passed away in his mid-nineties. Just a few months before he died, he was able to stand in the pulpit and preach once more at our church. Chester was a constant encourager to me. He would write me notes of encouragement every month or so, all typed on an old typewriter he used for his correspondence.

I'll never forget one note he sent me during a particularly challenging season in the life of our church. A couple of staff members had secretly recruited a number of our members to start a new church down the road, without my knowledge or blessing. This led to a splinter group leaving our church. Our staff was demoralized, and many in the church were discouraged. Many days during that season it was hard for me to get up and go to work. In the midst of that testing experience, Chester sent me one of his notes. He included at the end a poem written by Edgar A. Guest. I'd like to share it with you:

> It's the everlasting climbing
> that gets you to the top,
> And the everlasting sticking
> to the task you'd like to drop,
> It's the grit and vim and muscle
> In the rough and tumble tussle
> That will bring you home to victory
> and the distant goal you seek;
> It's the ever up and working
> Never lying down and shirking
> That eventually will land you
> on the mountain's sunny peak.[4]

Is this not what the author of Hebrews urges when he says, "Let us run with endurance the race that lies before us" (Heb. 12:1b)? Pastor, run the race of ministry well. Endure hardship. And "consider him who endured such hostility from sinners against himself, so that you won't grow weary and give up" (v. 3).

The Prophets Who Were before You

Jesus says that those who are persecuted should "be glad and rejoice" (Matt. 5:12). There are several reasons we can rejoice even in persecution. First, Jesus says the kingdom belongs to those who faithfully endure suffering for righteousness (v. 10). Second, he promises those who suffer well that their "reward is great in heaven" (v. 12a). Third, Jesus says that we can be glad and rejoice, "for that is how they persecuted the prophets who were before you" (v. 12b).

The last reason Jesus gives is of particular interest. Jesus is grounding the saints' rejoicing in suffering in the fact that they are participating in the same kind of suffering as the prophets of old. He is reminding us of the long line of faithful men and women on whose shoulders we stand. He is appealing to our memory. Remember, he says, those who came before you, and as you remember, rejoice.

When we consider history, we can gain valuable perspective on suffering and find hope as we seek to endure to the end. Hebrews 11 is one of the most insightful passages of Scripture for considering those who came before us. The author of Hebrews reminds us of those men and women of faith who trusted God and obeyed him "by faith." After listing men and women such as Abel, Enoch, Noah, Abraham, Sarah, Isaac, Jacob, Joseph, Moses, and Rahab, the author summarizes in Hebrews 11:32–39 the experience of some of the prophets:

> And what more can I say? Time is too short for me to tell about Gideon, Barak, Samson, Jephthah, David, Samuel, and the prophets, who by faith conquered kingdoms, administered justice, obtained promises, shut the

mouths of lions, quenched the raging of
fire, escaped the edge of the sword, gained
strength in weakness, became mighty in
battle, and put foreign armies to flight.
Women received their dead, raised to life
again. Other people were tortured, not
accepting release, so that they might gain
a better resurrection. Others experienced
mockings and scourgings, as well as bonds
and imprisonment. They were stoned, they
were sawed in two, they died by the sword,
they wandered about in sheepskins, in
goatskins, destitute, afflicted, and mistreated. The world was not worthy of
them. They wandered in deserts and on
mountains, hiding in caves and holes in
the ground.

All these were approved through their
faith.

These are "the prophets who were before you" (Matt.
5:12). This is what it looks like to endure persecution faithfully. What a legacy! "Time is too short," indeed, to discuss
the legacies of faithful men and women throughout the
generations of church history who have endured persecution, such as Anabaptists like Balthasar Hubmaier and
Michael Sattler; the Oxford martyrs Latimer, Ridley, and
Cranmer; and more recent martyrs such as Jim Elliott and
his associates.[5] We are heirs of this legacy, inheritors of a

history of faithful prophets who endured hardship for the sake of Christ's name.

There's a repeated refrain in the letters to the seven churches in Revelation. Seven times Jesus makes promises to "the one who conquers" (Rev. 2:7, 11, 17, 26; 3:5, 12, 21). Theologians refer to this call to "conquer" or endure to the end as *the perseverance of the saints*. This doctrine means that those who are genuinely converted to Christ will persevere in faith to the end.

The perseverance of the saints can be a daunting doctrine. However, this doctrine is undergirded by another: the doctrine of the *preservation of the saints*. The preservation of the saints means that God himself empowers our endurance. Peter says God not only gives us the gift of new birth but guards us by his power "through faith for a salvation that is ready to be revealed in the last time" (1 Pet. 1:3–5). That is, God not only redeems us; he *keeps* us. He not only saves us; he *sustains* us in faith. He not only rescues us; he *holds on* to us. He will never let us go. That's really the only hope we have of enduring through persecution. We can persevere because he preserves.

The preservation of the saints is a blessed doctrine. Yet there are further blessings for those who endure. Consider the promises Jesus makes to you if you endure to the end:

> He will give you "the right to eat from the tree of life" (Rev. 2:7).
>
> He will protect you from "the second death" (Rev. 2:11).

He will give you "some of the hidden manna" and "a new name" (Rev. 2:17).

He will give you "authority over the nations" and "the morning star" (Rev. 2:26–28).

He will give you "white clothes," your name will never be erased from the book of life, and you will be acknowledged before the Father (Rev. 3:5).

He will establish you permanently in God's presence, and you will bear his name (Rev. 3:12).

He will give you the right to sit with him on his throne (Rev. 3:21).

Our reward in heaven is great indeed. These promises for those who endure should motivate us to endure whatever hardship we experience as pastors. Look to the prophets' example and look for hope where they found it, in a faithful God who showers blessing after blessing upon us after preserving us to the end. Blessed are those who are persecuted.

Salt and Light

Before we leave this beatitude, I want to make one final observation. The thematic counterpart to this beatitude in the Sermon on the Mount is the "salt and light" text in

Matthew 5:13–16.[6] Jesus compares the disciples to salt that preserves and light that illuminates. He tells them: "Let your light shine before others, so that they may see your good works and give glory to your Father in heaven" (v. 16).

The thematic connection between the beatitude about enduring through persecution and Jesus' statement about salt and light is clear. He is describing the *result* of what happens when Matthew 5:10–12 is embraced. When we are willing to live righteously no matter the cost and are willing to endure persecution for our commitment to Jesus, it makes an impact in the culture around us. The way to be salt and light in the culture is to be so committed to Jesus that we are willing to follow him no matter what, even if it means walking the path of suffering.

Pastor, the stakes in ministry are high. It may just take your willingness to endure hardship "as a good soldier of Christ" (2 Tim. 2:3). Display your good works before others. For through this, someone may see that the gospel is really true, that God is really good, that you really believe what you preach, and give glory to God for it. Suffer well, pastor. Jesus is worth it.

PASTORAL REFLECTION

How to Withstand Criticism as a Pastor

– Mac Brunson –

Ministry and criticism go together. Where you find ministry, criticism is close behind. Moses was criticized repeatedly. David faced criticism: Shimei walked along the hilltop throwing rocks at David and cursing him continually (2 Sam. 16:5–8, 13). Nehemiah, a civil servant serving the Lord, faced criticism from without and from within. Even our Lord and Savior faced continuous criticism. He was criticized for his disciples not washing their hands, eating with sinners, and healing people on the Sabbath. The longer Jesus ministered, the sharper the criticism became.

At the beginning of his ministry, in the Sermon on the Mount, Jesus warned this was the result of living a life of righteousness. In reading the Beatitudes, you notice they are written in the third person: "Blessed are those. . . ." Matthew 5:10 begins that way but shifts to the second person by Matthew 5:11: "You are blessed when they insult you." Jesus comes and warns that those who are his disciples are going to face not just criticism but persecution as well.

Those committed to Christ today will find criticism abundant and public. The attacks are personal with a mixture of cruelty and anger. Critics always attempt to assign motives that are never there, breed discouragement, and focus on finding fault in everything. A critical spirit does not reflect the heart of God or the wise. Matthew 12:34b–35 says: "For the mouth speaks from the overflow of the heart. A good person produces good things from his storeroom of good, and an evil person produces evil things from his storeroom of evil."

In the Christian life you will have to learn how to face and handle criticism that comes your way. There are three principles to follow when dealing with critics.

The first way to handle critics and criticism is by prayer. Jesus, in the middle of this sermon, stopped and taught his disciples what we know as the Model Prayer (Matt. 6:9–13). In the heart of the prayer is the request for the Lord to forgive us our trespasses as we forgive those who trespass against us (v. 12). In Matthew 5:44, Jesus explicitly instructs his disciples to love their enemies and pray for those who persecute them. Part of what Jesus is teaching in this sermon is to deal with critics by praying and forgiving them.

The second way to handle criticism and critics is by persistence. Everything in Matthew 5:10–12 speaks of persistence, including the grammar. Jesus says, "Blessed are those who have been persecuted" (NASB). That is the passive perfect participle, and the perfect tense implies continuous action. There was a willingness on the part of his disciples to endure, to persevere even in the face of persecution. Never allow a critic to determine for you the length, the depth, or the width of God's ministry in you and through you. Persevere.

The third way to handle criticism and critics is through perspective. As much as anything in Matthew 5:12, Jesus is speaking of perspective. When you are insulted, when men speak evil of you, when you are persecuted, Jesus says "rejoice and be glad" (NASB). That is not an emotion. It is a choice. This is an imperative for the believer. This is not a matter of feelings, but a decision that you have made to rejoice and be glad in the midst of the criticism. Jesus tells us that our reward is in heaven (v. 12), and this is the perspective we are to have. Our future then is secure, and we stand in line with some of God's choicest of servants, the prophets.

Dealing with criticism and critics is never easy. It hurts, and we often carry those wounds around for a long time. However, the word of God says it is possible to face criticism and not just survive, but have victory.

CONCLUSION

The Blessed Pastor

"You are blessed. . . . Be glad and rejoice, because
your reward is great in heaven."

—Matthew 5:11–12

One of the features that stands out most prominently in the Beatitudes is the repetition of the phrase, "Blessed are." This changes in verse 11 to the simple, "You are blessed."

Blessed, recognizing our spiritual poverty. Blessed, being broken over our sin and humbled by it. Blessed, hungering and thirsting for the righteousness of Jesus. Blessed, becoming a person of mercy and purity who values peace among brothers and sisters. Blessed, enduring hardship for Jesus' sake.

These virtues are not flashy. In our culture, they are *strange*. It requires a certain going against the grain of what is considered normal. But they bring blessing. The pastor who embraces the character of Christ—that is to say, who allows God to form Christ's character in him—is a blessed pastor.

Being a pastor is one of the greatest blessings in my life. At the same time, it is one of the hardest parts of my life. Ministry can be both broken and beautiful. In what other vocation can you experience such amazing highs and lows in people's lives? Pastors are invited into the most intimate and precious moments of people's lives. We get to pray over new parents and their children. We get to be present when people put their faith in Christ and move from spiritual death to life. We celebrate baptism and spiritual growth markers in people's lives. We are at the hospital when they are sick. We sit near deathbeds and quietly sing and pray. We stand next to gravesides and weep with those who weep. We announce couple after couple as "husband and wife." What a blessing.

Ministry is sometimes a mixed blessing. At times, church members have hurt me. At times, they've helped me. They've been friends and foes. They've blessed and betrayed. They've brought provision into my life and sometimes opposition. Ministry is both a burden and a blessing. John Newton captured this tension well in his poem entitled "A Minister's Burden."

> What contradictions meet
> In ministers' employ!
> It is a bitter-sweet,
> A sorrow full of joy:

No other post affords a place
For equal honor or disgrace.

Who can describe the pain
Which faithful preachers feel,
Constrained to speak in vain,
To hearts as hard as steel?
Or who can tell the pleasures felt,
When stubborn hearts begin to melt?

The Savior's dying love,
The soul's amazing worth,
Their utmost efforts move,
And draw their bowels forth;
They pray and strive, the rest departs,
Till Christ be formed in sinners' hearts.

Pastoral ministry is indeed "a bitter sweet, a sorrow full of joy." Anyone who has pastored for any period of time at all knows that there is much bitterness and sorrow in ministry, but they also know the unique joys of ministry. Jesus refers to our joy in the Beatitudes.

Your Reward Is Great

The blessing of the Beatitudes leads us to joy. "Be glad and rejoice," Jesus says, "because your reward is great in heaven" (Matt. 5:12). This rejoicing because of our reward certainly refers to the immediate beatitude about persecution, but in another sense, it is a fitting conclusion to the

Beatitudes as a whole. The man or woman who embodies the Beatitudes has joy in a great reward.

Some people in church history have viewed the Beatitudes as an aspirational goal that believers aren't really expected to meet. Others have viewed the Beatitudes as a kind of "second law." Even if the Beatitudes are a kind of "law," James K. A. Smith gives us a helpful and hopeful word at this point:

> The law is seen as God's invitation to live a life of obedience out of gratitude; that is, God's law is not a stern restriction of our will but an invitation to find peace and rest in what Augustine would call the "right ordering" of our will. In this respect, the giving of commandments is an expression of love; the commandments are given as guardrails that encourage us to act in ways that are consistent with the "grain of the universe," so to speak. They are the means by which God invites and encourages us to find abundance and flourishing.[1]

Even if the Sermon on the Mount is a kind of restatement of God's law, it is still a gift of grace that leads to deep joy. If we understand the sermon properly, we will realize that the entirety of the Sermon on the Mount is not the description of a life lived under law at all, but the description of a life lived under and produced by God's grace. The sermon teaches that we must have righteousness that exceeds that of the Pharisees (Matt. 5:20) but that this is a righteousness *received* not *achieved*, as we first recognize our own spiritual bankruptcy (v. 3) and then hunger and thirst for God to fill us with *his* righteousness (v. 6). When read this way, the expectations and realities described in the Sermon on the Mount become not a hopelessly impossible standard to which we can never measure up, or a "law" that hangs over us and threatens to crush us, but rather a description of the life that has been transformed by Jesus. "Be glad and rejoice" (v. 12). The reward of the righteousness of Jesus' kingdom—his rule and reign in our lives—is indeed great.

This joy and this reward are not only available to disciples who live the "beatitudinal life," but also to those pastors who shape and form their ministries into the mold of the Sermon on the Mount. The pastor whose life reflects the Beatitudes can rejoice because his reward is great. Pastor, you need to know that Jesus is radically committed to your joy!

In 1 Peter 5, Peter speaks of a unique reward that faithful pastors receive. After encouraging pastors to shepherd the flock of God faithfully as "examples to the flock" (1 Pet. 5:2–3), Peter shares this promise: "And when the chief Shepherd appears, you will receive the unfading crown of glory" (v. 4). The word Peter uses for "crown" refers to the wreath that would have been placed on the head of an athletic champion, a soldier who had displayed courage in battle, or an emperor. Those wreaths would have wilted and faded over time, but the crown Jesus will give his pastors will never fade. It is a crown of *glory*, of recognition and approval by the King of kings and the Lord of lords. Pastor, the reward for a race well run is great.

The Promises of the Beatitudes

Jesus makes clear exactly what the blessings inherent in the life of the kingdom entail. The blessings are contained in the Beatitudes themselves as Jesus attaches promises to each one. Consider the eight Beatitudes once more, and look at the blessing of the promises Jesus makes in Matthew 5:3–12:

> "Blessed are the poor in spirit, *for the kingdom of heaven is theirs.*
>
> Blessed are those who mourn, *for they will be comforted.*
>
> Blessed are the humble, *for they will inherit the earth.*
>
> Blessed are those who hunger and thirst for righteousness, *for they will be filled.*
>
> Blessed are the merciful, *for they will be shown mercy.*
>
> Blessed are the pure in heart, *for they will see God.*
>
> Blessed are the peacemakers, *for they will be called sons of God.*

Blessed are those who are persecuted because of righteousness, *for the kingdom of heaven is theirs.*

"You are blessed when they insult you and persecute you and falsely say every kind of evil against you because of me. Be glad and rejoice, because *your reward is great in heaven.* For that is how they persecuted the prophets who were before you." (emphasis added)

Kingdom. Comfort. Inheritance. Filling. Mercy. Seeing God. Being called a son of God. Kingdom. These are the blessings of the Beatitudes. I love the way Eugene Peterson translates this section of the Sermon on the Mount in *The Message*. It captures the beauty of the promises Jesus makes:

"You're blessed when you're at the end of your rope. With less of you there is more of God and his rule.

"You're blessed when you feel you've lost what is most dear to you. Only then can you be embraced by the One most dear to you.

"You're blessed when you're content with just who you are—no more, no less. That's the moment you find yourselves proud owners of everything that can't be bought.

"You're blessed when you've worked up a good appetite for God. He's food and drink in the best meal you'll ever eat.

"You're blessed when you care. At the moment of being 'care-full,' you find yourselves cared for.

"You're blessed when you get your inside world—your mind and heart—put right. Then you can see God in the outside world.

"You're blessed when you can show people how to cooperate instead of compete or fight. That's when you discover who you really are, and your place in God's family.

"You're blessed when your commitment to God provokes persecution. The persecution drives you even deeper into God's kingdom.

"Not only that—count yourselves blessed every time people put you down or throw you out or speak lies about you to discredit me. What it means is that the truth is too close for comfort and they are uncomfortable. You can be glad when that happens—give a cheer, even!—for though they don't like it, *I* do! And all heaven applauds. And know that you are in good company. My prophets and witnesses have always gotten into this kind of trouble."

The pastor who embraces the life displayed in the Beatitudes is the blessed pastor. Ministry is a burden and a blessing, but when we minister with the character of Christ, there is a crowning reward. There's a blessing waiting for you when you go against the grain of modern ministry and shepherd like Jesus.

The Blessing of a Life of Ministry

– Hance Dilbeck –

On a warm summer night in August 1983, I walked an aisle at church camp to "surrender to the ministry." That's interesting language: "surrender to the ministry." It implies a certain reluctance. A soldier surrenders to the enemy; a criminal surrenders to the police; and a prospective pastor surrenders to his calling. I understand the language. To a certain point, it is valid. We embrace the role out of God's calling, not out of some lesser motive, but "voluntarily, according to the will of God," to use Peter's language (1 Pet. 5:2 NASB).

I have come to learn that this language of surrender, like all language, has its limits. "Surrender" seems to assume that the life of a pastor is all suffering and hardship. No one in his right mind would ever aspire to this work; no sane man would ever want to fill this role; he must be forced to bear the burden. Pastors do not enlist; they must be drafted!

I served as a pastor for thirty years. In the early years, I certainly felt forced into the role. However, I came to thrive under the yoke. As I look back on my life as a pastor, it is not the burdens but the blessings that stand out to me. I could touch on the blessings experienced by my family, but let me limit this testimony to the ways pastoral ministry blessed me personally. As a pastor, I was rooted, formed, and nourished.

Being a pastor forced me, and freed me, to sink my roots deep into the Word of God. You know the sayings: "Sundays come at the pastor like telephone poles come at the train." "Being a pastor is like having a baby every Sunday and finding out you're pregnant every Monday morning." Since it is always better to have something to say than to have to say something, the pastor must stay in the Word, "studying to show himself approved as a workman who rightly handles the word of God" (see 2 Tim. 2:15).

What a blessing to be called to devote yourself to prayer and the ministry of the Word. The weekly rhythm of sermon preparation, properly embraced, is a deep rhythm of personal discipleship. I am convinced that no one knows the Word like a God-called, Bible-preaching pastor. I am grateful for a lifetime of studying, understanding, and communicating the Bible. This work has blessed me with deep roots in God's Word.

Being a pastor formed me. When we do a work, we develop the capacity for that work. We build the muscles, we form the memories, we master the craft. To shepherd the flock of God shapes the heart of a man. To be a true shepherd, one must develop the mind of Christ. The Lord God is Shepherd, Jesus is Shepherd, and the pastor is shepherd.

I believe that thirty years of service under the chief Shepherd has made me more like Jesus. I love the church more like he loves her. I see people more like he sees them. I can endure hardship, forgive offenses, and extend grace in a way that I could not and

I would not if I had not done this work. Shepherding the flock of God made a shepherd out of me. Praise the Lord!

The local church has nurtured me. To nurture is to care for and encourage growth and development. The people of God have nourished and nurtured my gifts for the work. When I started, I was rough and weak. I was unrefined in my preaching ability. I lacked confidence and clarity in leadership. I bumbled and blundered through pastoral duties. Yet the people of God encouraged me. I can think of no better greenhouse for personal growth.

We pastors give those who hurt us more due than they deserve. In my experience, every mean-spirited deacon can be offset with dozens who were generous and gentle. Every complaint has been overwhelmed with a chorus of affirmation. I can think of no other vocation that encounters a steadier stream of kind words, thank-you notes, and Christmas gifts. The people of God love their pastors. What a blessing to serve people who will let you learn as you go, learning on the job. In a sense, the Lord called me to be a pastor, and the church made me to be a pastor. The people of God have nurtured me. For this, I give thanks.

Thirty years of shepherding the flock of God has been a blessing to me. In answering the call of God, I found a life rooted in the Word, formed by the work, and nurtured by God's people. "I thank Christ Jesus our Lord, who has strengthened me, because He considered me faithful, putting me into service" (1 Tim. 1:12 NASB).

About the Author

Andrew C. Hébert is the lead pastor of Paramount Baptist Church in Amarillo, Texas. He holds degrees from Criswell College and The Southern Baptist Theological Seminary. Andrew and his wife, Amy, have four children: Jenna, Austin, Mackenzie, and Brooklyn.

Notes

Foreword: What Is "Success" in Pastoral Ministry?

1. Hezekiah Harvey, *The Pastor: His Qualifications and Duties* (Philadelphia: American Baptist Publication Society, 1879), 164.

Chapter I: Pastoral (Bad) Attitudes

1. "Statistics in the Ministry," Pastoral Care Inc., accessed July 11, 2020, https://www.pastoralcareinc.com/statistics.

2. "The Porn Phenomenon," Barna Group, accessed on April 19, 2020, https://www.barna.com/the-porn-phenomenon/#.VqZoN_krIdU.

3. From David Ross's and Rick Blackmon's "Soul Care for Servants" workshop, reporting the results of their Fuller Institute of Church Growth research study in 1991 and other surveys in 2005 and 2006.

4. John McCallum, *The 23rd Pastor: Pastoring in the Spirit of Our Shepherd Lord* (self-pub., 2018), 49–50.

Chapter 2: Pastoral Beatitudes

1. Most books on pastoral ministry include a chapter or section on the pastor's character but rarely devote more to the subject. Two recent and refreshing exceptions are Paul David Tripp, *Dangerous Calling: Confronting the Unique Challenges of Pastoral Ministry* (Wheaton: Crossway Books, 2012), and Jeff Iorg, *The Character of Leadership: Nine Qualities that Define Great Leaders* (Nashville: B&H Publishing, 2007).

2. James N. Mattis and Francis J. West, *Call Sign Chaos: Learning to Lead* (New York: Random House, 2019), 11.

3. Charles H. Talbert, *Reading the Sermon on the Mount: Character Formation and Decision Making in Matthew 5–7* (Columbia, SC: University of South Carolina Press, 2004), 147–48.

4. James Montgomery Boice, *The Sermon on the Mount* (Grand Rapids: Baker Books, 1972), 15.

5. This insight was shared with me by Dr. H. LeRoy Metts, the brilliant longtime professor of Greek and New Testament at Criswell College in Dallas, Texas.

6. R. Kent Hughes, *The Sermon on the Mount: The Message of the Kingdom* (Wheaton: Crossway, 2001), 18.

7. A. M. Hunter, *Design for Life* (London: SCM Press, 1965), 34.

Pastoral Reflection: The "Well Done" in Ministry

1. "Statistics in the Ministry," Pastoral Care, Inc., accessed July 11, 2020, https://www.pastoralcareinc.com/statistics.

Chapter 3: The Spiritually Impoverished Pastor

1. D. A. Carson, *Jesus' Sermon on the Mount and His Confrontation with the World: An Exposition of Matthew 5–10* (Grand Rapids: Global Christian Publishers, 1987), 18.

2. William Willimon, *Pastor: The Theology and Practice of Ordained Ministry* (Nashville: Abingdon Press, 2002), 23.

3. I originally wrote parts of this section for *For the Church*, the online resource site of Midwestern Baptist Theological Seminary, in an article entitled "Embracing Accusation." The original article can be accessed here: https://ftc.co/resource -library/blog-entries/embracing-accusation, accessed April 24, 2020.

4. See the structural outline on pages 37–38.

Chapter 4: The Broken Pastor

1. This is commonly attributed to Spurgeon, however it hasn't been found in any of his published sermons; https:// www.spurgeon.org/resource-library/blog-entries/6-quotes -spurgeon-didnt-say/.

2. William Barclay, *The Gospel of Matthew*, vol. 1 (Philadelphia: Westminster Press, 1958), 95.

3. R. Kent Hughes, *The Sermon on the Mount: The Message of the Kingdom* (Wheaton: Crossway Books, 2001), 29.

4. Thomas Watson, *The Doctrine of Repentance* (Edinburgh: Banner of Truth, 1988), 63.

5. John Claypool, *The Preaching Event* (Waco, TX: Word Books, 1980), 86.

6. See the structural outline on pages 37–38.

7. Claypool, *The Preaching Event*, 86–87.

Pastoral Reflection: The Repentance Is for the Redeemed

1. William H. Willimon and Richard Lischer, eds., *Concise Encyclopedia of Preaching* (Louisville, KY: Westminster John Knox Press, 1995), 517.

2. Martin Luther, *The Ninety-Five Theses and Other Writings*, edited and translated by William R. Russell, (New York: Penguin Books, 2017), 3.

Chapter 5: The Humble Pastor

1. Dr. Dew's full message can be viewed here: https://www.youtube.com/watch?v=vLSzGsqGQf8, accessed May 4, 2020.

2. Andrew Roberts, *Napoleon: A Life* (New York: Penguin Books, 2015), 355.

3. C. S. Lewis, *Mere Christianity* (San Francisco: HarperOne, 2015), 128.

4. Eugene Peterson, *The Pastor: A Memoir* (New York: HarperOne, 2011), 292.

5. Kevin Vanhoozer and Owen Strachan, *The Pastor as Public Theologian: Reclaiming a Lost Vision* (Grand Rapids, MI: Baker Academic, 2015), 13.

6. See the structural outline on pages 37–38.

7. C. S. Lewis, *The Weight of Glory* (San Francisco: HarperOne, 2001), 36.

8. Lewis, *The Weight of Glory*, 41.

9. Lewis, *The Weight of Glory*, 42.

Chapter 6: The Hungry Pastor

1. A. W. Tozer, *The Pursuit of God* (Harrisburg, PA: Christian Publications, 1948), 11–12.

2. Martin Luther, *Luther's Large Catechism*, trans. John Nicholas Lenker (Minneapolis: Luther, 1908), 44.

3. James K. A. Smith, *You Are What You Love: The Spiritual Power of Habit* (Grand Rapids, MI: Brazos Press, 2016), 9. Emphasis in original.

4. See the structural outline of the Sermon on the Mount on pages 37–38.

5. Eugene Peterson, *Working the Angles: The Shape of Pastoral Integrity* (Grand Rapids, MI: Eerdmans, 1987), 15.

6. Peterson, *Working the Angles*, 3–4.

Pastoral Reflection: The Pastor's Time with God

1. Mariano Di Gangi, *The Meaning of Christian Discipleship* (Agincourt, Ontario: Bible & Medical Missionary Fellowship, 1975).

Chapter 7: The Sympathetic Pastor

1. Names have been changed to protect their privacy.

2. William Willimon, *Pastor: The Theology and Practice of Ordained Ministry* (Nashville: Abingdon Press, 2002), 317.

3. N. T. Wright, *Matthew for Everyone: Part Two, Chapters 16–28* (Louisville, KY: Westminster John Knox Press, 2004), 39–40.

4. See the structural outline on pages 37–38.

5. Harold L. Senkbeil, *The Care of Souls: Cultivating a Pastor's Heart* (Bellingham, WA: Lexham Press, 2019), xxi.

6. Tim Keller, *Ministries of Mercy: The Call of the Jericho Road* (Phillipsburg, NJ: P&R Publishing Company, 2015), 30.

Chapter 8: The Pure Pastor

1. "Chocolate Allergies Linked to Cockroach Parts," NBC News, April 2, 2012, accessed June 18, 2020, https://www.nbcnews.com/healthmain/chocolate-allergies-linked-cockroach-parts-628784#:~:text=According%20to%20ABC%20News%2C%20the,the%20Food%20and%20Drug%20Administration.

2. David Christie, *The Service of Christ* (London: Hodder and Stoughton, 1933), 66.

3. See the structural outline of the Sermon on the Mount on pages 37–38.

Chapter 9: The Reconciling Pastor

1. S. Truett Cathy, *Eat Mor Chikin, Inspire More People: Doing Business the Chick-fil-A Way* (Decatur, GA: Looking Glass Books, 2002), 77. Emphasis in original.

2. Jonathan Edwards, "Pastor and People Must Look to God," in *The Salvation of Souls: Nine Previously Unpublished Sermons on the Call of Ministry and the Gospel*, eds. Richard Bailey and Gregory Wills (Wheaton, IL: Crossway, 2002), 142.

3. William Raymond Manchester and Paul Reid, *The Last Lion: Winston Spencer Churchill*, vol. 3 (New York: Bantam Books, 2013), 950.

4. Joel Gregory delivered this message during the 1988 Southern Baptist Convention Annual Meeting. His message can be accessed at https://www.youtube.com/watch?v=MMyEU l8B4No&t=8s, accessed June 25, 2020.

5. Albert Mohler, "A Call for Theological Triage and Christian Maturity," July 12, 2005, accessed June 25, 2020, https://albertmohler.com/2005/07/12/a-call-for-theological-triage-and-christian-maturity?fbclid=IwAR3kB00dBCVC

GRAS1llyTfzrXv2mwSyIniOHizSXwXfp12UMRFlUWha
EZ-o. I would also recommend Gavin Ortlund, *Finding the
Right Hills to Die On: The Case for Theological Triage* (Wheaton,
IL: Crossway, 2020), and Rhyne R. Putman, *When Doctrine
Divides the People of God: An Evangelical Approach to Theological
Diversity* (Wheaton, IL: Crossway, 2020).

6. Ken Sande, *The Peacemaker: A Biblical Guide to Resolving
Personal Conflict* (Grand Rapids, MI: Baker Books, 2004), 98.

7. Alan Jacobs, *How to Think: A Survival Guide for a World
at Odds* (New York: Currency, 2017), 110.

8. Jacobs, *How to Think*, 147.

9. Jacobs, *How to Think*, 62.

10. This anecdote came from a letter from Barry Stricker
to John Shouse, February 7, 2018. It is included in Chris Chun
and John Shouse, *Golden Gate to Gateway: A History* (Nashville:
B&H Publishing Group, 2020), 76.

11. See the structural outline for the Sermon on the Mount
on pages 37–38.

12. Charles Williams, *He Came Down from Heaven and The
Forgiveness of Sins* (Berkeley, CA: Apocryphile Press, 2005),
145.

Chapter 10: The Enduring Pastor

1. Kenneth C. Haugk, *Antagonists in the Church: How to
Identify and Deal with Destructive Conflict* (Minneapolis, MN:
Augsburg Press, 1988), 22–23.

2. John McCallum, *The 23rd Pastor: Pastoring in the Spirit of
Our Shepherd Lord* (self-pub., 2018), 110.

3. R. Kent Hughes, *The Sermon on the Mount: The Message of
the Kingdom* (Wheaton, IL: Crossway Books, 2001), 71.

4. Edgar A. Guest, *The Passing Throng: Today and Tomorrow* (Chicago: The Reilly & Lee Company, 1923), 72.

5. If you want to gain encouragement from the stories of some of these faithful martyrs, I recommend William R. Estep, *The Anabaptist Story* (Nashville: Broadman Press, 1963); Harold J. Chadwick, *Foxe's Book of Martyrs*, John Foxe, ed. (Newberry, FL: Bridge-Logos, 2001); and Richard Wurmbrand, *Tortured for Christ* (Bartlesville, OK: Living Sacrifice Book Company, 1998).

6. See the structural outline on pages 37–38.

Conclusion: The Blessed Pastor

1. James K. A. Smith, *Desiring the Kingdom: Worship, Worldview, and Cultural Formation* (Grand Rapids, MI: Baker Academic, 2009), 174–75.